T0333895

THE MYTH OF
MEASUREMENT

SAGE SWIFTS SERIES

The **SAGE SWIFTS** series showcases the best of social science research that has the potential to influence public policy and practice, resulting in positive social change. We strongly believe that the social sciences are uniquely positioned to make this impact and thus benefit society in a myriad of ways.

SAGE SWIFTS celebrate and support the impact of quality empirical work that provides a provocative intervention into current debates, helping society to meet critical challenges going forward.

TITLES IN THE SERIES INCLUDE:

RANK HYPOCRISIES
THE INSULT OF THE REF
DEREK SAYER

THE CRISIS OF PRESENCE IN CONTEMPORARY CULTURE
VINCENT MILLER

UNIVERSITIES AT WAR
THOMAS DOCHERTY

MISOGYNY ONLINE
A SHORT (AND BRUTISH) HISTORY
EMMA A. JANE

CULTURAL RELATIVISM AND INTERNATIONAL POLITICS
DEREK ROBBINS

INTERCULTURAL CITIZENSHIP IN THE POST-MULTICULTURAL ERA
RICARD ZAPATA-BARRERO

THE MYTH OF MEASUREMENT

INSPECTION, AUDIT, TARGETS AND THE PUBLIC SECTOR

NICK FROST

Los Angeles | London | New Delhi
Singapore | Washington DC | Melbourne

Los Angeles | London | New Delhi
Singapore | Washington DC | Melbourne

SAGE Publications Ltd
1 Oliver's Yard
55 City Road
London EC1Y 1SP

SAGE Publications Inc.
2455 Teller Road
Thousand Oaks, California 91320

SAGE Publications India Pvt Ltd
B 1/I 1 Mohan Cooperative Industrial Area
Mathura Road
New Delhi 110 044

SAGE Publications Asia-Pacific Pte Ltd
3 Church Street
#10-04 Samsung Hub
Singapore 049483

Editor: Kate Keers
Assistant editor: Catriona McMullen
Production editor: Manmeet Kaur Tura
Copyeditor: Gemma Marren
Proofreader: Derek Markham
Marketing manager: Camille Richmond
Cover design: Wendy Scott
Typeset by: C&M Digitals (P) Ltd, Chennai, India
Printed in the UK

Library of Congress Control Number: 2021938336

British Library Cataloguing in Publication data

A catalogue record for this book is available from
the British Library

ISBN 978-1-5297-3266-5
eISBN 978-1-5297-6074-3

At SAGE we take sustainability seriously. Most of our products are printed in the UK using responsibly sourced paper
and boards. When we print overseas we ensure sustainable papers are used as measured by the PREPS grading
system. We undertake an annual audit to monitor our sustainability.

CONTENTS

LIST OF TABLES

ABOUT THE AUTHOR

Nick Frost is Emeritus Professor of Social Work at Leeds Beckett University. He is formerly a social worker and adult educator. Nick has written or edited more than 20 books and has been involved in chairing a number of public and voluntary organisations. He is the author, most recently, of Safeguarding Children and Young People (Sage, 2021).

AUTHOR'S ACKNOWLEDGEMENTS

I would most of all like to thank the public sector workers who struggle, often against the odds, to provide high quality services for their service users. I am grateful to those I interviewed about their experiences of inspections and audits. Many thanks to Nigel Parton and Richard Skues for their specialist advice. Thanks also are due to the excellent editorial team at SAGE.

PUBLISHER'S ACKNOWLEDGEMENTS

The author and the publisher are grateful for permission to reproduce the following material in this book:

Chapter 2, excerpt from Cui, V., French, A. and O'Leary, M. (2019) A missed opportunity? How the UK's teaching excellence framework fails to capture the voice of university staff, *Studies in Higher Education*. Copyright © Society for Research into Higher Education, reprinted by permission of Taylor & Francis Ltd, www.tandfonline.com.

Chapter 4, excerpt from Vainikainen, M.P., Thuneberg, H., Marjanen, J., Hautamäki, J., Kupiainen, S. and Hotulainen, R. (2017) How do Finns know? Educational monitoring without inspection and standard setting. In Blömeke, S. and Gustafsson, J.E. (eds), *Standard Setting in Education: The Nordic Countries in an International Perspective*. Cham: Springer, pp. 243–259. Reprinted by permission of Springer Nature.

INTRODUCTION

The Mayor: I have called you together, gentlemen, to communicate to you a most unpleasant piece of news: an Inspector is coming to visit us … Our visitor is pretty certain to want to inspect the charitable institutions under your supervision first of all, so take care that everything is as it should be: see that the nightcaps are clean and that the patients don't look like sweeps, as they do on an ordinary day.

Gogol, *The Government Inspector* – first performed in Russia in 1843

A team of school inspectors – smartly dressed and carrying their bags of laptops and papers – walk up the path of an urban primary school. The school secretary, a local woman, is expecting the team, welcomes them and asks the team if they would take a seat whilst she finds the headteacher. The headteacher soon arrives and reaches out to shake the hand of the inspectors only to be told: 'we regret to inform you that the inspection has been discontinued, due to poor safeguarding practice'. The headteacher is shocked and asks why? The Lead Inspector replies, 'because the school secretary failed to ask us for identification': the inspection team left. Urban myth? I thought so too until the episode was later verified by the local Director of Children's Services.

These and other comparable narratives stimulated me to ask a series of questions about the role and function of inspection and audit regimes. Why did a range of professionals I know, across a variety of organisations, worry so much about the forthcoming inspection? Why did organisations and leaders I respected obtain so-called inadequate judgements? Why did my place of work, of which I had a very positive experience, regularly appear in the lower places of various league tables? Were the resources and effort dedicated to the inspection and measurement task justified?

The origins of this book, and my direct involvement as an object of inspection and audit, lay in these questions and observations. This book therefore aims to explore the background, development, techniques and the impact of such inspection and audit regimes in five areas of the public sector. Organisations explored here include: schools, universities, police forces, children's services and health services: all are people-centred, human service organisations. They are – in the main – publicly funded and thus are subject to varying forms of political and public accountability. Accountability in the private sector is mainly to shareholders but also to regulatory bodies – where there may be some resemblance to the issues raised here.

I draw on a number of sources: I have interviewed two senior professionals in each field, a total of ten semi-structured interviews. I have studied a number of key theoretical and research-based studies: these are outlined and analysed in Chapter 1. Further, I have read many of the relevant key performance indicators, league tables and inspection reports relevant to the organisations studied: material which will be drawn upon as the argument unfolds. I use 'audit culture' as a form of shorthand for all forms of inspections, audits, league tables and measurement of public service organisations.

It is claimed that inspection and audit regimes have many advantages: they provide a form of public accountability, allow citizens to evaluate the quality of public sector organisations, employ skilled and experienced professionals and encourage organisations to improve their performance. I agree with elements of this argument but the aim of the book is to provide a counter-argument where three central propositions are made:

1. Audit culture is based on a lack of trust in public service professionalism and has undermined what used to be seen as the public service ethos.

2. Audit culture produces proxy measures which become fetishised and can have a negative impact on service delivery.

3. The attempt to 'quantify' the 'quality' of public service organisations is expensive, diversionary, leads to gaming and can cause distress to many well-motivated professionals.

It is hoped that taken together these propositions make a persuasive critical argument for the rethinking and reform of public accountability mechanisms and techniques. The book explores both forms of measurement, audits and inspections, as 'the difference between audits and inspections cannot simply be defined' (Power 1997: 129).

I felt that it was incumbent for the book to suggest some alternative mechanisms for ensuring service improvement and public accountability, as George Monbiot (2019) argues, when dominant narratives are challenged we require alternative forms of narrative. This is discussed in the Chapter 7. The aim is to suggest a framework that is fairer, kinder and more appropriate in ensuring effective forms of public accountability.

1

MEASURING EVERYTHING IN THE PUBLIC SECTOR

This chapter introduces the debates around the central issues explored through-out the book and presents the primary proposal of the book that inspection and audit culture should be reformed and improved to have a more positive impact upon the public sector. The chapter begins by exploring the existing literature, outlining the growth and development of audit and inspection. The three central arguments will be made:

1. Audit culture is based on? a lack of trust in public service professionalism and has undermined what used to be seen as the public service ethos.

2. Audit culture produces proxy measures which become fetishised and can have a negative impact on service delivery.

3. The attempt to 'quantify' the 'quality' of public service organisations is expensive, diversionary, leads to gaming and can cause distress to many well-motivated professionals.

The inspector has a long history: the first Her Majesty's Inspectors of Schools were introduced in England in 1839, for example. They feature in classic works of fiction such as Gogol's *The Government Inspector* (1843) and in a number of Charles Dickens' novels. There is no doubt that many aspects of life can be measured, scored and assessed: the profit figures produced by a company are probably (putting to one side the quirks of accountability and tax avoidance techniques) accurate, the number of patients admitted to a given hospital in a given month can be measured, as can the number of arrests in a week in a defined police area. There is clearly a role for measurement and statistics in assessing public services, thus, it is not intended to argue here that facts do not exist, nor that reality cannot be measured. Hans Rosling, for example, provides excellent examples of the use of facts and statistics in the ground-breaking book *Factfulness* (2018). But how can quality, as opposed to quantity, of public service be measured? Can we tell which is the highest quality university or school or hospital?

Think about the following everyday events from public sector practice:

A social worker supports a distressed young person who is feeling suicidal and succeeds in enabling the young person to see the positives in their life.

A police officer supports a victim of sexual crime over a period of months.

A teacher delivers an inspirational lesson to a group of disaffected 15 year olds.

A lecturer provides a session that challenges and stimulates a group of students.

A doctor offers a listening ear to a distressed patient.

How can we measure these powerful, relationship-based, inter-personal events? I am reminded of interviewing a refugee Somalian mother about her experiences of a children's centre: she stated that 'I used to cry alone, now I have many shoulders to cry on'. Such a response is immeasurable and cannot be assessed by the gaze of the auditor. Writing about performance management in the private sector Redden argues that such techniques are 'concerned with quantification of quality' (2019: 16) and Lipsky points out that 'there really are few valid statistics where the quality of performance is at issue' (1980: 52). There is therefore a complex and contested relationship between audit culture and the assessment of quality: 'the well-recognised problem of defining objectives and performance for public services whose outputs are difficult to identify' (Power 1997: 114).

All the organisations explored in this study depend on their frontline staff to deliver services: the academics, social workers, teachers, health and medical staff and police officers whose work is discussed here. In his classic text, Michael Lipsky describes these staff as 'street-level bureaucrats', defining them as:

Public sector workers who interact directly with citizens in the course of their jobs, and who have substantial discretion in the execution of their work. (1980: 3)

Lipsky's book is complex and deeply insightful. He argues that in relation to statistics and quality: 'It is not even apparent whether measured increases or decreases signal better or worse performance' (1980: 50). We are, of course, dependent on these staff to deliver our services. Writing in 1980 Lipsky further argued that:

> we *must* have people making decisions and treating people in the public services. We are not yet prepared as a society to abandon decisions about people and discretionary intervention to machines and programmed formats. (1980: xv)

Whilst data and technology have developed since Lipsky was writing, this point remains a forceful one. On occasions when decisions are left to machines this can backfire: the English Secretary of State for Education, Gavin Williamson, came under considerable criticism when he did just this and allowed an algorithm to determine the A-level results during the COVID-19 crisis of 2020 (Cowburn 2020). He soon reversed his decision.

Lipsky states, in an argument consistent with the approach of this book, that:

> Job performance in street-level bureaucracies is extremely difficult to measure. The many implications of this statement include the facts that these agencies are not self-corrective, and the definition of adequate performance is highly politicised. (1980: 48)

Lipsky also introduces some of the key themes of this book. For example, he analyses the relationship between audit techniques and professional behaviours as follows:

> Confronted with more clients than can readily be accommodated, street-level bureaucrats often choose ... those who seem most likely to succeed in terms of bureaucratic success criteria. (1980: 107)

Lipsky also discusses the impact of audit techniques on organisational behaviour:

> In the current period bureaucratic accountability policies also have negative consequences because of competing demands on, and of, administrators. (1980: 170)

These issues will be illustrated in the five case studies that form the core of this book.

One of the key arguments here is that quality cannot be measured in statistical terms. Authorities therefore create proxy measures such as: the number of visits made by a social worker, a decline in the crime rate or an increase in the examination pass rate, which in turn become ways of measuring complex and nuanced events. For example, the quality of university teaching is measured through the National Student Survey (NSS) score: students provide a scaled response to a number of questions about their courses. The quality of a given lecture is difficult to measure through a score: would a 10 mean a lecture was intellectually challenging or simply easily digestible by the audience? Thus, in the UK university courses are measured through a score given by Year Three students: which excludes Year One, Year Two, Masters and other postgraduate students – this measure is therefore a proxy of wider quality, a quality which is difficult to capture. As Lipsky argues:

> Street-level bureaucracies attempt to promote the validity of surrogate measures to the general public in an effort to appear accountable through performance measures. (1980: 52)

METHODOLOGY UNDERPINNING THIS BOOK

This books offers a critical commentary on the role of the audit culture in public service. Five case studies are offered, one in each of Chapters 2, 3, 4, 5 and 6. The case studies are of the universities, the National Health Service, schools, children's social care and policing. The content of this book draws primarily from three sources:

1. Social theory: major texts exploring organisational theory, accountability, auditing, social statistics.

2. Official audit and statistical sources: inspection reports, statistical data, league tables and supporting documentation.

3. Interviews: ten semi-structured interviews were undertaken with senior staff from the five organisational streams that are explored. Respondents were recruited using snowball methods. Informed consent was obtained, interviews were recorded and transcribed: recordings were then deleted. All respondents are anonymised and no identifying data is utilised: direct quotes, checked back with the respondents, are utilised in the five case studies. Table 1.1 outlines the interviews undertaken.

Table 1.1   Case studies undertaken for this study

Organisation	Audit regimes	Interviewees
NHS	Care Quality Commission Targets Outcome data	Senior consultant . Two senior nurses (one joint interview)
Schooling	Ofsted League tables Outcome data	Teacher (1) Teacher (2)
Children's Services	Ofsted Joint inspections Outcome data	Senior manager (1) Senior manager (2)
Police	Her Majesty's Inspectors Targets Independent Office for Police Conduct	Senior police officer (1) Senior police officer (2)
Universities	League tables Research Excellence Framework Teaching Excellence Framework Office for Students	Senior academic (1) Senior academic (2)

There is no claim here that this is a representative sample. I simply wanted to give a voice to a selection of professionals on these issues that have such an impact on their working lives: their voice is rarely heard on these important issues. The book quotes from them extensively and uses their narratives to steer and inform the argument and analysis.

PERFORMING WITHIN AN AUDIT CULTURE

Foucault's work on surveillance, classification and measurement is highly suggestive in helping us reflect on the role of the State, organisations and how professionals perform under inspection and audit regimes. Foucault suggests that in modern societies classification and measurement are techniques of exercising power. Foucault names this as governmentality:

> an activity that undertakes to conduct individuals throughout their lives by placing them under the authority of a guide responsible for what they do and for what happens to them. (1997: 68)

Foucault explains how these forms of power operate:

> We must cease once and for all to describe the effects of power in negative terms: it 'excludes', it 'represses', it 'censors', it 'abstracts', it 'masks', it 'conceals'. In fact power produces: it produces reality: it produces domains of objects and rituals of truth. The individual and the knowledge that may be gained of him [sic] belong to this production. (1997: 194)

Miller and Rose's discussion of these issues can be clearly related to audit culture:

> The term governmentality sought to draw attention to a certain way of thinking and acting embodied in all those attempts to know and govern the wealth, health and happiness of populations. Foucault argued that, since the eighteenth century, this way of reflecting upon power and seeking to render it operable had achieved pre-eminence over other forms of political power. It was linked to the proliferation of a whole range of apparatuses pertaining to government and a complex body of knowledges and 'know-how' about government, the means of its exercise and the nature of those over whom it was to be exercised. (1992: 272)

An aspect of these techniques is that the objects of the audit gaze themselves partake in the process and become agents within these processes, something our respondents reflect upon in the interviews utilised in our case studies. Redden reflects upon this as follows:

> Data fosters calculative practices, calculative entities and calculating agents, and also calculative sociality among those seen as responsible for determining how to create measurable outcomes of value. (2019: 11)

Thus, if I am reading these complex ideas correctly, audit processes create human beings who measure, who calculate and who want to succeed in the pursuit of positive outcomes. The professionals studied in this book want the audit techniques to work and they want to be successful in the terms of the audit; sometimes, as we shall see, these roles are performed at great personal cost. Redden places this in a political context and explores how audit cultures have a divisive impact:

> through performing differential impact of persons and entities – Performance Management facilitates the competitive sociality associated with neo-liberal rationalities that have dominated government and business. (2019: 9)

Such examples will be provided in this book – in particular in Chapter 5. The growth of audit culture cannot be separated from wider social and political changes.

Organisational leaders, working within audit cultures, wish for the positive inspection outcome above all else. They buy in to the system and measure themselves and others according to the last inspection outcome, as evidenced throughout this study:

> Power is not so much a matter of imposing constraints upon citizens as of 'making up' citizens capable of bearing a kind of regulated freedom. Personal autonomy is not the antithesis of political power, but a key term in its exercise, the more so because most individuals are not merely the subjects of power but play a part in its operations. (Miller and Rose 1992: 272)

People who are otherwise excellent critical thinkers completely immerse themselves in the inspection game. They spend months preparing, they continually expect the inspection to be 'next week' and they generate files full of data. They designate lead officers, run mock exercises and prepare scripts for all levels of workers: the inspection game is played to the full. This is the dream of governance and audit systems: the subjects of inspection buy into the system and co-operate in full. The inspection outcome therefore becomes the symbol, the goal and the ultimate measure of success. As Mike Power argues:

> The ideal form of surveillance is the totally observed and known individual who ends up as a self-observing and self-disciplining agent. (1997: 128)

Miller and Rose elaborate as follows:

> Central to the possibility of modern forms of government, we argue, are the associations formed between entities constituted as 'political' and the projects, plans and practices of those authorities – economic, legal, spiritual, medical, technical – who endeavour to administer the lives of others in the light of conceptions of what is good, healthy, normal, virtuous, efficient or profitable. Knowledge is thus central to these activities of government and to the very formation of its objects, for government is a domain of cognition, calculation, experimentation and evaluation. (1992: 272)

They further argue that the focus should not be on mechanisms of social control but on the way citizens are encouraged, persuaded, induced and motivated to act in a particular way towards particular goals.

The inspection process can be seen as a drama – an event with a beginning, a middle and a conclusion. It has a script, a narrative and a predictable, or sometimes an unexpected ending. Mike Power argues that 'auditing has the character of a certain kind of organisational script whose dramaturgical essence is the production of comfort' (1997: 123), to which I would add forms of discomfort as well. The analogy with drama is powerful as the actors are provided with scripts and attend rehearsals. I was once involved in a local authority faced with significant expenditure cuts (known as 'savings' for the inspection period) – my script was not to mention funding as the inspectors would think 'we aren't managing the savings'. The most significant challenge of resources was not part of the script and not supposed to be mentioned during the inspection process. Thus the inspection has its own narrative – with sometimes a tenuous link with reality, another issue mentioned by our respondents throughout this study. The eminent sociologist Erving Goffman (1978) would relate this to the presentation of self: the way we manage impressions and how others view us. The inspection therefore succeeds in making the objects of inspection active participants in the process, totally immersed in a process of judgement and assessment: complicit in the entire process and sometimes even in negative outcomes. Audit cultures therefore have an inter-personal, social and psychological aspect – the making of active participants in a process of measurement, assessment and outcomes. They also have an organisational and political aspect, which is the primary subject of Mike Power's classic text *The Audit Society*, published in 1997, and worthy of extended exploration as it provides many of the underpinning arguments of the current text.

Power, himself once a practising financial auditor, provides a social constructionist critique of auditing. His key argument is that 'methods of checking and verification are diverse, sometimes perverse, sometimes burdensome, and always costly' (1997: 1). He places his analysis of the public sector with the context of the New Public Management, which he sees as 'the desire to replace the presumed inefficiency of hierarchical bureaucracy with the presumed efficiency of markets' (1997: 43). These processes provide a need for accountability that is played out through an explosion of audit techniques, which 'represents a decision to shift evaluative cultures away from social scientific towards a managerial knowledge base' (1997: 67). Mike Power sees this as 'a huge and unavoidable social experiment which is conspicuously cross-sectional and trans-national' (1997: xv). He refers to the expansion of audit culture and how these processes are rarely subject to critical examination:

> The audit explosion represents a systematic shift from the logic of evaluation to that of auditing, a shift which puts auditing itself beyond evaluation. (Power 1997: 115)

For Power, the audit culture is the ultimate arbiter and is rarely challenged and questioned. Given Power's background in financial auditing it is particularly interesting that he argues that 'evidence is not just out there ... evidence is always relative to the rules of acceptance for particular communities' (1997: 69). I take this to be a social constructionist approach that informs the analysis here: inspection and audit techniques are constructed by social processes – they do not just exist out there in some objective, scientific form. Many of the respondents in this study are clearly aware of the contested nature of inspections – using words such as random, lucky and variable. Power argues that:

> For auditing practitioners 'making things auditable' is a deeply practical issue. It is what they do when they apply various techniques, routines and experiences to an organisation. This process is not a science: it is largely a matter of practitioner commonsense and intuition. (1997: 87)

For Power, audits are seen as 'rationalised rituals of inspection', which result in particular forms of challenge, reassurance, accountability and legitimacy. Drawing on Foucault, Power argues that professionals can welcome forms of audit and proportionate monitoring as evidence of successful results and of documentary proof of their activities: 'audit requires not just an auditable reality but one which reflects institutional myths about the appropriate level of formality' (1997: 99). Audits perform a useful task, they make 'activities less heterogenous, less complex and less uncertain' (1997: 121).

As Power implies, inspection and audit systems are underpinned by lack of trust. If we had trust in our social institutions the whole audit process would collapse: why invest millions in a process of inspection audit if trust existed? The seventeenth-century village would have total trust, and indeed deference, towards their local teacher, doctor and vicar. Trust displaces the need for audit and inspection. As Onora O'Neill argues:

> Like many of us, I live and work among professionals and public servants. And those whom I know seek to serve the public conscientiously – and mostly to pretty good effect. Addenbrooke's, for example, is an outstanding hospital: the University of Cambridge and many surrounding research institutions do distinguished work: Cambridgeshire schools, social services and police have good reputations. Yet during the last fifteen years we have all found our reputations and performance doubted, as have millions of other public sector workers and professionals. We increasingly hear that we are no longer trusted. (2002: 43)

If we lend a good friend £10 during a night out we do not feel the need to set up an audit system: we trust them to repay, although failure to do so may undermine some of that trust. If we had trust in all our professions then there would be no need for expensive and resource-heavy audit regimes. As Mike Power writes:

> Changes which have taken place in the public sector in recent years reflect institutionalised distrust in the capacity of teachers, social workers, and university lecturers to self-regulate the quality of their services. (1997: 135)

Whilst 'professionalism may be characterised in part by the self-control of quality' (Power 1997: 103) there are of course good reasons not to trust some professionals – in the UK we can think of the names of Harold Shipman, Beverly Allitt and Ian Paterson, all trusted health professionals who undertook seriously harmful behaviours – and we can see why we need accountability and disciplinary systems, an issue we return to later.

A primary purpose of this book is to make the case for the reform of the inspection system and audit of public bodies. The reader may assume that inspection is 'a good thing' as it assures quality in public services. This is partly the case, but there are challenges inherent in the issue of inspection. A case example is provided here to set the scene for the rest of the book and to present some of the key challenges: the aim is to illustrate how the inspection process is socially constructed. The section that follows is perhaps the most powerful case for such reform: it concerns the London Borough of Haringey during the period 2006–2008, which is most notorious for the sad death of a little boy who became known as 'Baby P' (Jones 2014). In 2006, prior to the death of Baby P, the Borough was subject to a Joint Review – the then current system by which Children's Services were inspected. The inspection was generally positive. Eleven judgements were made that were all 'good' or 'adequate', with none being either 'outstanding' or 'inadequate'. The report stated, for example, that:

> Outcomes in Haringey have improved measurably in the last five years, in most cases in line with national trends, and in many cases at a faster rate than nationally and in similar authorities. This progress reflects the improving quality of services and the collective will across the council and its partners to raise standards in all areas. (Ofsted 2006: 4)

Soon after this, the death of Baby P occurred and the case attracted perhaps the highest ever media and political profile of any child death. As a result of this the then Secretary of State, Ed Balls, asked Ofsted to undertake a further, emergency inspection. The outcome of the report provides a powerful contrast to the previous report:

This inspection has identified a number of serious concerns in relation to safe-guarding of children and young people in Haringey. The contribution of local services to improving outcomes for children and young people at risk or requiring safeguarding is inadequate and needs urgent and sustained attention. (2008: 3)

Table 1.2 below compares and contrasts the two reports undertaken in 2006 and 2008 respectively.

Table 1.2   Comparing two inspections: Ofsted inspections of Haringey 2006 and 2008

Issue	2006 report	2008 report
Child protection	Child protection work is generally of a satisfactory standard; most performance indicators are now in line with those in comparator authorities. This reflects good and sustained improvements in practice and management since 2001 when practice was poor. All children on the child protection register have an allocated social worker and cases are reviewed within timescales. (Page 18)	This inspection has identified a number of serious concerns in relation to safeguarding of children and young people in Haringey. The contribution of local services to improving outcomes for children and young people at risk or requiring safeguarding is inadequate and needs urgent and sustained attention. (Page 3)
Leadership	The ambitions established by the council and its partners for children and young people in Haringey are good. The CYPP 'Changing Lives' links clearly to the Every Child Matters outcomes and is ambitious and challenging. The plan is based on an extensive analysis of shared needs founded on well-presented data and evidence from a range of sources, including a health equity audit. The needs of vulnerable groups are highlighted well and the actions needed to address gaps in service provision reflect the diversity of the community. (Page 27)	There is a managerial failure to ensure full compliance with some requirements of the inquiry into the death of Victoria Climbie, such as the lack of written feedback to those making referrals to social care services. (Page 3)

(Continued)

Table 1.2   (Continued)

Issue	2006 report	2008 report
LSCB	The LSCB, which was established well in advance of the national deadline, works to the pan-London child protection procedures. It has established an ambitious programme and good ownership of the wider safeguarding agenda with procedures in place to review serious incidents. A newly integrated child protection unit, composed of child protection advisers from social care and education, supports the LSCB and multi-agency working. Links between the LSCB and the voluntary sector are good and developing further. (Page 19)	The local safeguarding children board (LSCB) fails to provide sufficient challenge to its member agencies. This is further compounded by the lack of an independent chairperson. (Page 3)
Multi-agency working	The capacity of the council and its partners to improve further services for children is good. The director of the children's service provides strong and dynamic leadership and is supported by many examples of good leadership and management at all levels. The lead member has a clear understanding of her role and responsibilities, building well on the previous involvement and commitment of the leader of the council. Partners share a strong vision for the development of the children's service and in recent years have demonstrated. (Page 29)	Social care, health and police authorities do not communicate and collaborate routinely and consistently to ensure effective assessment, planning and review of cases of vulnerable children and young people. (Page 3)
Assessments	The majority of assessments of need are undertaken in a timely way. In recent years, a high proportion of initial assessments have been made in response to referrals, reflecting an understandably cautious approach to protecting children. (Page 18)	Too often assessments of children and young people, in all agencies, fail to identify those who are at immediate risk of harm and to address their needs. (Page 3)

Issue	2006 report	2008 report
Frontline practice	Staff are well managed and supported to carry out their roles, and improvement in the quality of social work practice in care proceedings has been recognised by local courts. General and specialist child protection training for all relevant staff, including voluntary sector partners is very good, is valued by staff and improves the quality of child protection work. (Page 18)	The quality of frontline practice across all agencies is inconsistent. (Page 3)
Performance management	Performance management is good. There is a clear commitment to, and focus on, improving performance by both councillors and officers; scrutiny arrangements are secure. The performance management framework is good and is used consistently across the children's service, except in the youth service. Performance management reports are good and used widely in the children's service and with partners. Performance reports are produced monthly for managers and these are shared with frontline staff. Local performance indicators have been developed and are used well to track performance on local priorities. As a result, the council and its partners have a good understanding of performance against their ambitions and priorities. (Page 29)	Arrangements for scrutinising performance across the council and the partnership are insufficiently developed and fail to provide systematic support and appropriate challenge to both managers and practitioners. (Page 4)
Use of data	The CYPP 'Changing Lives' links clearly to the Every Child Matters outcomes and is ambitious and challenging. The plan is based on an extensive analysis of shared needs founded on well-presented data and evidence from a range of sources, including a health equity audit. (Page 27)	There is too much reliance on quantitative data to measure social care, health, and police performance, without sufficiently robust analysis of the underlying quality of service provision and practice. (Page 4)

It is absolutely lacking in credibility that such a negative overall change could have been taking place in only two years (see Jones 2014). The first Ofsted report is generally positive in tone, whilst making some recommendations for change and improvement. The second report, following a strong political intervention, is damning in tone and damaged the career of the Director of Children's Services – who later went on to win court proceedings against her unfair dismissal. As argued earlier, this is an illustration of how the inspection process can be flawed and what is dressed up in the language of objectivity and science is actually politicised, socially constructed, subjective and can be driven by agendas outside of any neutral assessment of 'quality'.

DEMOCRACY, ACCOUNTABILITY AND PUBLIC SECTOR DELIVERY

One hallmark of liberal democracy is that it promotes forms of public accountability at all levels of public administration. In totalitarian societies public organisations – most notably the police, the army and the secret service – are only accountable internally and perhaps to a dictator. The consequences of such regimes are well known in states such as Communist-era East Germany (Dennis and Laporte 2014). Some form of accountability is, therefore, desirable in liberal democracies to protect citizens' rights against unjust decision-making and even arbitrary arrest. In this context accountability attempts to ensure that professionals do not abuse their power and that services are provided to at least a minimum level of quality. This accountability is complex and varied: it ranges through parliamentary elections, public access to local authority meetings, inspections, the publication of performance data and the role of the media. As Warren puts it, there exist:

> vast and complex webs of accountabilities between peoples and those who govern on their behalf and in their name. (2014: 39)

Mike Power notes the transformation from large, state-led provision to systems of procurement and competitive tendering as follows:

> As the welfare state becomes displaced by the regulatory state, instruments of audit and inspection become even more central to the operations and identity of politicians and identity of governments and politicians. (1997: xii)

These shifts have placed accountability centre stage: Dubnick argues that 'accountability has truly become a golden concept' (2014: 25) and demonstrates this empirically, noting a dramatic increase in the use of the term in academic literature since the 1960s. For Lipsky, 'accountability is the link between bureaucracy and democracy' (1980: 152), an issue we return to in our final chapter. Certainly the culture of audit and measurement has grown, due to:

> The extraordinarily rapid expansion in the scale, scope and intensity of inspection of public services which has taken place in the UK … since the 1970s. (Martin and Davis 2008: 13–14)

In her 2002 BBC Reith lectures O'Neill makes a similar point:

> And in the last two decades, the quest for greater accountability has penetrated all our lives, like great draughts of Heineken, reaching parts that supposedly less developed forms of accountability did not reach. (2002: 45)

The audit explosion has been underpinned by new forms of managerialism and leadership thinking, largely drawn from the private sector:

> In 1986 the American management guru, Tom Peters, embraced the motto, 'what gets measured gets done', which became a cornerstone belief of metrics. In time, some drew the conclusion that 'anything that can be measured can be improved'. (Muller 2018: 17)

Jerry Muller notes this explosion and highlights some of the issues and challenges:

> The metric fixation is the seemingly irresistible pressure to measure performance, to publicise it, and to reward it, often in the face of evidence that this just doesn't work very well. Used properly, measurement … can be a good thing. So can transparency. But they can also distort, divert, displace and discourage … we live in an age of mismeasurement, over-measurement, misleading measurement, and counter-productive measurement. (2018: 4)

Power makes a similar point:

> The audit explosion contains many dangers and the concept of an audit society suggest the pathologicality of excessive checking. (1997: xii)

In terms of the concerns of this book, accountability largely is concerned with ensuring that professionals (social workers, teachers, medical professionals, police officers and academics) do not abuse their professional skills and power base and that they deliver high quality services. The most acute case concerns police officers where the dangers of arbitrary arrest are clear, but we also want to know that a doctor is not privileging one patient over another, or a teacher is not over-marking the work of a favourite pupil, for example.

There are various levels of trust, accountability and risk at play here:

- *Implicit trust*: We may trust a doctor because they are a doctor – an Ipsos Mori survey in 2020 suggested that trust in doctors was 91% and in nurses was over 93%. (Ipsos Mori, Veracity Index 2020). This form of trust is situated in forms of deference where a citizen defers to a professional because of the prestige they have by being a member of that profession and possessing the relevant professional skills and knowledge. Many Victorian novels demonstrate trust in the local vicar, doctor or teacher that follows from their knowledge and authority. These forms of trust have changed in recent decades as deference has changed, trust in experts has been questioned, individualism has increased and various 'scandals' have contributed to a decline in trust. It is difficult to state that one would always trust a GP after the Harold Shipman case or always trust a police officer after the Stephen Lawrence murder, for example. There would also be an interplay between the profession in general (all GPs for example) and our own direct experience of our own, local GP. So it would be possible to state, 'I do not trust GPs in general but I trust my GP, who has served me well in the past'.
- *Democratic trust*: We may trust people because they have been elected – the President, the mayor or the local councillor, for example. By voting for them we have delegated a leadership task to this person, perhaps demonstrating a form of trust. We hope they will be accountable and trustworthy as they may ask us to vote for them again in the future. This form of delegated trust has severe limitations. For example, we may know little about, say, the Police and Crime Commissioner, and therefore our trust would have little basis in fact. We may also feel that an election of a mayor in three years' time is a very weak form of accountability. The Brexit referendum in the UK in 2016 reflected some of these factors: a majority seemed not to trust the experts (of the Confederation of British Industry, the Trades Union Congress or the Bank of England) and felt that the election of a Member of the European Parliament did not generate sufficient democratic accountability.
- *Bureaucratic accountability*: Organisations have systems, measurements and methods – issues are checked and signed-off by senior staff. As O'Neill writes: They require detailed conformity to procedures and protocols,

detailed record-keeping and provision of information in specified for-mats and success in reaching targets. Detailed instructions regulate and prescribe the work and performance of health trusts and schools, of uni-versities and research councils, of the police force and of social workers. (2002: 46)

This is perhaps the main concern of this book: what is the fit between follow-ing procedures and the generation of trust. Do I trust the local primary school to educate my child when it has been graded as inadequate by Ofsted? Do I trust my local police force to investigate a burglary when their clear up rate is the lowest in the country? The citizen would have to be well informed to reach these judgements: a position enhanced in the digital age, where the citizen can access information through the web. I argue at various points in this book that this transparency is often opaque, to say the least. Both the university-based Transparency Approach to Costing (TRAC from here on) system and the performance data of consultants in the NHS are difficult to locate and arguably very difficult to interpret in a manner that might influence citizen choices, as demonstrated later in this book. The generation of external measures and targets undermines trust as explained by Taylor-Gooby who argues that:

> Competitive and target driven approaches direct provider interests outwards to the market or upwards to the target setter and away from the needs of the service user. Trust becomes vulnerable. (2009: 106)

GAME PLAYING AND INDUSTRIAL DEVIANCE

One of the great silent issues of modern public service is that professionals know that inspections and forms of audit are flawed and inaccurate but this is largely unspoken and rarely systematically challenged. In Chapter Two we discuss an example from the university sector where academic staff are asked to complete a form known as TRAC – where they allocate their work time to pre-defined categories. We argue that the data gathered is probably highly inaccurate but it is collated and published and becomes a form of truth. Completing the form inaccurately is an example of what can be identified as workplace deviance:

> Workplace deviance refers to voluntary behaviour in that employees either lack motivation to conform to, and/or become motivated to violate, normative expectations of the social context. (Bennett and Robinson 2000: 349)

All my respondents were either wary of, or felt vulnerable towards, the systems of inspection and audit in their specific professions: as a result they often played the system. As Lipsky argues:

> Managers try to restrict workers' discretion in order to secure certain results, but street-level bureaucrats often regard such efforts as illegitimate and to some degree resist them successfully. (1980: 19)

As we will see throughout this book some measures can be 'gamed': professionals know what is being measured and can, therefore, target this measure for improvement, perhaps to the detriment of other areas of practice, for example, by concentrating high quality teaching on the brightest pupils to boost examination grades. As O'Neill argues:

> I think that many public sector professionals find that the new demands damage their real work. Teachers aim to teach their pupils: nurses to care for their patients: university lecturers to do research and to teach: police officers to deter and apprehend those whose activities harm the community: social workers to help those whose lives are for various reasons unmanageable or very difficult. Each profession has its proper aim, and this aim is not reducible to meeting set targets. (2002: 49)

AUDIT REGIMES: REAL COSTS, OPPORTUNITY COSTS AND UNINTENDED CONSEQUENCES

In his vital book in this field of study Jerry Muller (2018) has argued that metrics are costly and generate a number of organisational behaviours, including 'gaming through creaming', by which professionals work on more straightforward cases, where targets can be met more easily, whilst excluding more complex and demanding cases. Further Muller argues professionals can aim at 'improving numbers by lowering standards', for example, by reducing the criteria for assessing the work of students, or by travel companies increasing scheduled journey times, thus making it easier to hit punctuality targets. They may also aim at 'improving numbers through omission or distortion of data': ignoring difficult cases, or by classifying cases differently, or by not recording certain crimes, for example. Muller's final illustration of how metrics distort practices he calls, quite simply, 'cheating', quoting evidence of student marks being altered following the incentives introduced by the No Child Left Behind Act in the United States (Muller 2018: 25).

Muller argues that all public sector audit regimes suffer from various forms of these challenges. In addition audit regimes are, of course, not cost free:

> detractors argue that it places a huge bureaucratic burden on inspected services and diverts resources from frontline service delivery. (Davis and Martin 2008: 7)

We analyse the costs of audit using three measures: actual costs, opportunity costs and unintended consequences. The actual costs of inspection regimes are substantial. Ofsted, for example, cost more than £136 million during the financial year 2019–2020. In addition we should factor in the preparation costs of organisations prior to inspection, staff time during inspections and implementation costs after inspections. I am unaware of any studies or estimates of such costs but they are no doubt substantial.

There are of course also opportunity costs – when people are engaged in inspections they are not undertaking other tasks. Educationalists working for Ofsted are not teaching, police professionals working for the HMICFRS are not undertaking policing and so on. This also applies to the staff within organisations who spend their time preparing for inspections. So the investment of time and money into inspection and audit detracts from actual professional time dedicated to direct work with citizens whose lives are affected by the organisations discussed in this book.

Finally, and it is argued here most significantly, there are the unintended consequences of inspection. As Lipsky argues:

> Street-level bureaucracies encounter conflict and ambiguity in the tensions between client-centred goals and organisational goals. (1980: 44)

Unintended consequences occur where otherwise successful careers are undermined, organisational reputations are destroyed and costs are incurred through subsequent redundancies and reorganisations. An example, which occurs regularly in children's social care, is where an authority (Authority A) is found to be inadequate, due to social work related matters. Authority A will then attempt to recruit extra experienced social workers through golden handshakes and enhanced pay grades. This may well result in social workers moving from Authority B to Authority A – leading to staffing shortages at Authority B, and perhaps in turn leading to poor inspection outcomes. This is a negative impact of inspection and audit regimes: ironically this is often reported on in Ofsted inspections. The unintended consequence is that local authorities are often sent into turmoil following negative inspection findings. The cycle will often go as follows:

- negative inspection findings
- negative local and sometimes national media coverage
- departure of senior staff
- haemorrhaging of frontline staff
- recruitment of temporary senior managers on high day rates (often in excess of £1,000 per day)
- recruitment of agency frontline staff
- structural reorganisations
- recruitment of new senior leadership teams.

It is then hoped that a period of stability follows. Evidence for this process is provided later in this book.

CONCLUSION

This chapter has attempted to provide the context and theoretical framework for the remainder of the book. It has presented the main critical challenges that will be evidenced in the five case studies that follow. Each case study provides material relevant to each specific organisation and is informed by quotes from our respondents. The final chapter of the book attempts to bring together the main themes, addresses the three core arguments and suggests a way forward to a fairer, more empathetic, kinder and more equitable way of working with public services to ensure quality, fairness and participation in these essential services. We are arguing for more humane, flexible and empathetic audit regimes which recognise that:

> Street-level bureaucrats often work in situations too complicated to reduce to programmatic formats … [they] often work in situations that require human responses to the human dimensions of situations … street-level discretion promotes workers' self-regard and encourages clients to believe that workers hold the key to their well-being. (Lipsky 1980: 15)

2

ASSESSING QUALITY IN UNIVERSITIES: MEASURING TEACHING AND RESEARCH

This opening case study explores the state of play in British universities which have, since the 1960s, moved from being relatively autonomous and independent bodies to being subject to rigorous and demanding audit regimes – including the Research Excellence Framework (REF), the Teaching Excellence Framework (TEF), the National Student Survey (NSS) and the production of numerous league tables. They are subjected to, perhaps, the most varied, multi-levelled and diverse forms of the audit gaze of all the institutions explored in the five case studies. The impact of these audit regimes will be analysed in this chapter, the core argument being that the use of metrics is not helpful in gauging quality and their use simply reproduces and reflects an elitist higher education system. As in our other case studies, two experienced respondents were interviewed to inform the analysis. The author has 20 years' experience of working in universities and I draw significantly on my own experience.

Traditionally, the university has prided itself as being independent in thought and autonomously organised and led – 'academic freedom', as defined below, was greatly valued:

> the freedom of teachers and students to teach, study, and pursue knowledge and research without unreasonable interference or restriction from law, institutional regulations, or public pressure. Its basic elements include the freedom of teachers to inquire into any subject that evokes their intellectual concern: to present their findings to their students, colleagues, and others: to publish their data and conclusions without control or censorship: and to teach in the manner they consider professionally appropriate. For students, the basic elements

include the freedom to study subjects that concern them and to form conclusions for themselves and express their opinions. (www.britannica.com/topic/academic-freedom)

This autonomy allowed universities to undertake original, and sometimes even oppositional research, and teaching. The outstanding British historian and political activist E.P. Thompson was so concerned by the undermining of this independence when he perceived the influence of commercial interests emerging throughout the 1960s that he produced the book *Warwick University Limited* (1970). Thompson argued that commercial interests were undermining concepts of academic freedom and independence. He asks:

> Is it inevitable that the university will be reduced to the function of providing, with increasingly authoritarian efficiency, pre-packed intellectual commodities which meet the requirements of management? (1970: 166)

In the 2020s Thompson would now undoubtedly perceive that the changes he feared have come to be. Universities now share many of the features of other neo-liberal institutions, including:

- highly paid leaders
- internal markets
- teams of auditors, accountants, data analysts and change teams
- reliance on key performance indicators
- existing as a 'market' serving 'consumers'.

As Rowan Moore puts it, universities:

> now have to act, to a much greater degree than before, like businesses, competing to attract the highest number of students and the income that comes with them, as well as maximising their revenue from other sources and reducing their costs. They market and advertise and pay high salaries to senior executives. In principle they can merge and acquire, and they can go bust. These changes are called 'marketisation' and 'commodification', especially by those who oppose them. (Moore 2021)

The eminent and highly readable commentator on these issues, Stefan Collini, comments as follows:

> unless the case is made in terms which governments and taxpayers recognize, we risk 'shooting ourselves in the foot'. But what this involves, at least in part,

is employing categories and descriptions which we know, or ought to know, misrepresent the true purpose and value of much of what is done in universities. And this is one source of the malaise that now afflicts so many academics in countries such as Britain. (2012: 94)

Thus we have seen a shift from fairly autonomous, intellectual and creative centres to competitive, market-led, tightly audited bodies. There is a key tension here: academics wish to live in an environment of academic freedom, free to work and think as they wish, but they are in turn dependent on public money, research funding and student fees for their livelihood, so have to be accountable either through a market or through a form of bureaucracy. This tension has been settled in the current era through the dominance of an audit and metrics regime.

One of the respondents disagreed with my analysis here and argues that:

There is no contradiction between academic freedom and accountability, the two things are completely different. Academic freedom is to hold unpopular opinions and to be free from harassment, but you are not free to be a lousy teacher! (Respondent Two)

This point is taken, but it is argued here that the regime of quality control and the various techniques of measurement and audit in universities create an environment of performance and monitoring that sits uncomfortably with academic freedom. Discussions of REFs and TEFs dominate management practices, water cooler discussion and filter down to everyday practices, thus governing the performance of academics. For example, I was once (mistakenly) advised by a Dean, wanting to maximise the REF score, not to write any more books as they were not valued by the REF system – strange advice indeed to an academic! This is just one example of many of how the audit gaze percolates into day-to-day practice.

TIME AND MOTION IN UNIVERSITIES

One of the great largely unspoken issues of modern public service is that professionals know that inspections and forms of audit are flawed and inaccurate, but they are obliged to be fully engaged in these processes and find the regimes difficult to resist and contest, as argued in Chapter 1. To provide an example, university academic staff are required to complete a TRAC form. Version 4.2 of the guidance consists of 149 pages and explains the purpose of TRAC as follows:

> The full economic cost (fEC) is the cost which, if recovered across an organisa-tion's full programme, would recover the total cost: direct, indirect and an ade-quate investment in the institution infrastructure and future productive capacity. It is important that costs reported under TRAC better reflect the full long-term costs of maintaining the institution's infrastructure in a safe and productive state, and to a standard that reflects the norm required to be competitive in the sector. (OfS 2019: 60)

One can note the language of the market here: economic cost, investment, productive capacity and competitive. The report could refer to a widget factory or call centre. No mention is made of public sector values, learning or social purpose, thus demonstrating how the language of competition displaces pub-lic sector values and thinking. TRAC is elaborated upon as follows:

> The aim is to ensure institutions have a TRAC process that is overseen and gov-erned in a way that promotes material accuracy and the importance and useful-ness of the results. The governance and quality assurance arrangements seek to reduce the likelihood of material errors and/or erroneous judgements being made. In turn this aims to provide confidence and assurance to internal and external stakeholders and funders, through the production of robust and reasonable information. (OfS 2019: 24)

The main activities that staff are asked to allocate their time between are as follows:

- Teaching (T) – analysed between publicly and non-publicly funded activity
- Research (R) – analysed between the main sponsor types: Research Councils, Government Departments, charities, European Commission bodies, etc.
- Other (O) – the other primary income-generating activities such as com-mercial activities, residences, conferences
- Support activities (S) – such as preparation, proposal-writing and adminis-tration, which are costed separately but are attributed, as appropriate, to the three core activities – Teaching, Research and Other. (OfS 2019: 6–7)

For the individual staff member the process involves allocating working time to a number of boxes as a percentage – for example 15% publicly funded teach-ing, 10% funded research, 20% for support and so on until the total is 100%. One of my respondents stated, and many others have said to me informally, 'I make mine up: everyone makes them up!'. To complete the TRAC form accurately would indeed be a Herculean task – every ten minute phone call, five minute corridor chat with an anxious student and idle gossip over coffee would require recording and categorising. Of course no one does this, unless they happen to be in a job that coincides 100% with one of the boxes, and thus the data generated is therefore certainly inaccurate. All this inaccurate data is then collated, signed-off institutionally and then published nationally. This data is transformed from rough and ready guess work by thousands of busy academics and becomes a solid representation of some sort of 'reality'. It is a process where the actors are obliged to participate (if you fail to fill in the form you will receive a series of reminders), and institutions will be seen as failing if they do not participate. The central drivers create a culture of compliance to produce an over-simplified picture of something that is actually complex and largely intangible. One of my respondents summarised their experience of TRAC as follows:

> You have to map how you spend your time – I never saw any outcomes from it, nor was I sure of the purpose. It felt like a bureaucratic exercise without a rationale. It was hard to disaggregate the data – it was just not accurate. I couldn't disaggregate what fitted into each category – it was all very confusing. (Respondent One)

The other respondent is equally critical:

> TRAC is not useful, and not realistic. It was simple for me, as I had a single role – general support for teaching 100%, so it took me 30 seconds to fill it in. In general it was completely meaningless as it is was not possible to calculate and parcel activities up to percentages of time. The job description could do this task: that would be the closest we could ever get. When you aggregate all the individuals it is an accumulation of nonsense. We just had to do it and there was never any feedback: we never heard that this was useful. You just did it and forgot about it. There was no managerial oversight of this, to shield people so they report what they actually do. The futility of the exercise was made to appear meaningful. (Respondent Two)

I randomly sampled five university websites to explore the transparency issue represented by the T in TRAC. I found no published reports of single institution TRACs. Three of the searches came up with results for TRAC – these referred to meeting minutes that had mentioned approved TRAC returns, but I could find no discussion of implications of the returns. Two searches found pro-forma TRAC returns – but these were behind fire walls and were not accessible to members of the public or researchers. It is difficult therefore to sustain the transparency argument around TRAC. Obviously a more extensive exploration could take place but I suspect the results would be similar to those drawn from this small sample. There is a dedicated TRAC website which provides extensive guidance, aggregated data and a TRAC pro-forma: again I could not find any institutional data. The TRAC process produces extensive aggregated data from which the headline seems to be that universities undertake research at a deficit.

Thus I conclude this discussion of TRAC as follows:

- TRAC is an expensive exercise which takes a considerable amount of academic and administrative time.
- TRAC collates a large amount of data that is most probably inaccurate.
- Institution-based TRAC data is not transparent to the public.

UNIVERSITY LEAGUE TABLES

Universities vary in their history, aims and purpose: each is unique and exists in a specific historical and social space. In the United Kingdom some universities date back to medieval times (Oxford is the oldest university, being founded in 1096), some were designated as polytechnics and became universities in 1992, others gained their charter even more recently. As a result partly rooted in their history, partly due to their current funding and their purpose, universities are very different: league tables are an attempt to compare and assess them through shared metrics. They are highly significant as they:

> possess the aura of both precision and objectivity and so, when joined with the assumption about competition, can generate a definitive ranking. Vice-chancellors now keep as nervous an eye on league tables as do football managers, and placings are frequently invoked to legitimate a preferred policy shift. (Collini 2012: 17–18)

There are many forms of university league tables – here we draw on the example of those drawn up by the well-regarded and influential *Guardian* newspaper in the United Kingdom. 121 universities are ranked – one of my former institutions came 106th in 2021 – an issue I will reflect on further later in this chapter. The *Guardian* league table (www.theguardian.com/education/universityguide) aggregates the following metrics:

- the percentage of students satisfied with their course, gathered from the National Student Survey (NSS)
- the percentage of students satisfied with teaching, gathered from the National Student Survey (NSS)

- the percentage of students satisfied with feedback on their coursework, gathered from the National Student Survey (NSS)
- student-to-staff ratio – with lower scores rated better
- spend per student – scored out of 10
- the average entry tariff
- a value-added score out of ten – comparing entry scores with degrees achieved
- the number of students working in degree level jobs, 15 months after graduation
- the continuation rate – the percentage of students transferring from Year One to Year Two.

This is a complex mix of consumer feedback, expenditure and other measures, which in true metric style are reduced to a single score – 100 for Oxford at the top through to 30.1 for Bedfordshire at the bottom. The actual real differences are complex and difficult to analyse. For example, 80.6% of students at the London School of Economics (positioned 5th), are satisfied with their course, compared to 84.5% at the West of Scotland (positioned 120th). Value-added at third placed Cambridge is scored at 5, compared with an equal value-added score at lowly De Montfort University (119th). Durham (4th) and London Metropolitan University (118th) share identical spend figures. The only figure that seems to consistently reflect the position in the league table is the tariff entry score: it ranges from 212 for Cambridge (3rd) to 96 for London Metropolitan University (118th). These figures are arguably circular in effect – the tariff reflects tradition, reputation, positions in league tables and related status, which in turn allows higher tariff entry scores. The league table for the United Kingdom is thus highly predictable – I can confidently predict that Oxford, Cambridge, the London School of Economics, Imperial, St Andrews and Durham will be in the top ten in any version of league tables. The social good represented by the widening participation policies of say Bedfordshire, London Metropolitan and others are punished by low positions in the tables, as one respondent commented:

> The league tables are basically nonsense. We were always near the bottom of all of the league tables and again this drove central management initiatives: overall it was not a very good thing. We wanted to move up and become average. You can inch up but it is complete nonsense, due to real-world constraints. Certain things can be done but everyone is trying to move up if possible, so the gains are marginal. There is a rough correlation between all the tables with the same universities in the top 20 and the bottom 20: within that the positions may vary.

[There is] no reason to think the variation is real. I think the variation is random and an artefact of the process. (Respondent Two)

The misplaced use of league tables is reflected upon by Collini as follows:

In this way, discussion of universities, as of many other matters, has become afflicted with 'Champions League syndrome'. It is assumed that all the 'top' universities 'play' in the same 'league' – I deliberately make the quotation marks intrusive to call attention to the misleadingness of these familiar metaphors. (2012: 18)

The other respondent reflects how metrics dominate leadership teams:

League tables have a huge importance amongst executive teams as they are high profile in the public domain. (Respondent One)

The respondent also raises the issue of the provider/consumer model. The league tables, like the other metrics aimed at enhancing consumer choice, assume the rational consumer who is free to move anywhere in the country. In reality, a student who is, say, a parent dependent on extended family for child care, that choice is an illusion. One respondent felt that:

I am not sure that league tables lead to informed choices for students. (Respondent One)

A similar argument is made by Rowan Moore:

New breeds of consultants have grown up, 'a coterie of corporate experts' as Amelia Horgan of the University of Essex puts it, to help universities maximise their intakes, sell themselves and raise their ratings but there remains a deep flaw in the idea that you can have a free market in higher education, which is that a degree course is not like a can of baked beans, where you can try out different brands to find which one you like. (Moore 2021)

The league tables reflect the dangers of metrics – reducing complexity to digits, assessing quality in quantitative terms. Personally, having worked at a so-called 'top 20' and a 'bottom 20' university, I would rate the latter as more positive in every way. If one can be allowed an illustrative anecdote: I came across a top 20 university that was issuing a reading list to students that was 10 years out-of-date – something that I never saw at my lowly bottom 20 university.

As Collini comments, the whole idea of league tables sits uncomfortably with the purpose of universities:

> Another problem arising out of the analogy I'm discussing is that businesses which make a similar product are necessarily in competition with each other. But this is only true in a metaphorical sense for universities: scholarship is in fact an inherently *cooperative* enterprise. (Collini 2012: 140)

The audit culture has generated competition in an environment that should be co-operative.

THE NATIONAL STUDENT SURVEY

The issue of student engagement and the subsequent urge to measure this is an international issue:

> The emergence of student engagement as a significant strand of research into higher education contexts may be explained largely by reference to rising participation rates on an international basis at a time of increasing marketization of the university sector … These twin forces have led governments to be increasingly concerned about completion rates and levels of student achievement as a means of demonstrating value for money from public and private investment. This, in turn, has increased demands on institutions in respect to monitoring and reporting of relevant data. (Macfarlane and Tomlinson 2017: 5)

Cheng and Marsh have produced an extensive critique of the theory and practice of student engagement surveys and conclude that:

> at the university level, there are relatively few universities that differ significantly from the mean across all universities and, at the course level, there is even a smaller portion of differences that are statistically significant. This suggests the inappropriateness of these ratings for the construction of league tables. (2010: 709)

Each year universities undertake a National Student Survey (NSS from here on). The survey is of final year undergraduates and asks them to assess the quality of their courses using a Likert scale. There is an incentive to achieve the highest possible returns and as a consequence universities encourage students to complete the survey, as argued by Rowan Moore:

> [the NSS] performs the ostensibly valuable task of asking students what they think of their courses, but is a bete noire of many academics. Their complaint

is partly about the imposition of yet more bureaucratic procedure on their and their students' time – 'we have to badger our students to get them to bloody well do it', says the architecture professor, 'we have an event with free pizza, chips and beer to get them to fill in the forms.' Metrics, he also says, are 'a very poor way of describing what is really going on'. (Moore 2021)

There are other incentives too as evidenced by a notice I witnessed in a Law School clearly encouraging students to give high scores in the NSS, as this would enhance the reputation of the course and in turn improve the career opportunities of the students. This provides a clear example of gaming the system.

One of my respondents felt strongly about this issue, arguing against turning quality into quantity as follows:

> At the micro-level it has struck me as very odd when you talk about Academic Quality, given it is called Academic Quality there is an awful lot of quantity that goes into it. This quantification is at the heart of the academic system, like marking. Students want the quantitative mark but this is antithetical in coming to grips with the quality of their work and with the qualitative feedback. This applies to degree classifications too … The quality industry is a misnomer too – as it is quantified, it is what the quality industry does. The idea that you can quantify something like quality when it can't be standardised – it is a perversion just to do it: it is a contradiction. (Respondent Two)

As with many of the metrics explored in this book, Rowan Moore argues that this system can be gamed as follows:

> One of the most significant factors in students' happiness is the grades they get in their exams, which incentivises universities to mark them higher, which contributes to a grade inflation that has seen first-class degrees rise from 16% of the total in 2010–11 to 30% in 2018–19, while the proportion of those gaining either a first or a 2:1 has climbed from 67% to 79%. Several academics tell stories of receiving very strong hints from management that they should raise the marks they award. (Moore 2021)

In addition, the NSS only explores the views of final year undergraduates: thus excluding undergraduates at other stages of their programme and postgraduates. The NSS therefore has significant drawbacks and provides a poor proxy for real student experiences. One of the respondents summarises this well:

> The Likert scales turn quality into quantity – it is a misnomer, in the NSS quality is numbers. (Respondent Two)

RESEARCH EXCELLENCE FRAMEWORK

Perhaps the single most extreme example of 'the myth of measurement' covered in this book comes in the form of the Research Excellence Framework (REF). The REF is a process of assessing the quality of the research in British universities: it has a number of tiers and reaches a final judgement in the form of a league table, with higher scores attracting extra funding. The link between the process and funding allocation is questioned by Collini:

> There is still the fundamental question of why a department whose research happens to get taken up in this way should be any more highly rated (and rewarded) than one which does not. Not only do a variety of uncontrollable factors determine the chances of such translation to another medium, but there is also no reason to think that the success of such translation bears any relation to the research quality of the original work. (2012: 172)

One of the methods, and arguably the highest profile, is to assess research outputs (books, papers and other outputs) of academics. Thus a paper published in a journal, for example, would be given a score as follows, according to the REF guidance:

- Four star: Quality that is world-leading in terms of originality, significance and rigour.
- Three star: Quality that is internationally excellent in terms of originality, significance and rigour but which falls short of the highest standards of excellence.
- Two star: Quality that is recognised internationally in terms of originality, significance and rigour.
- One star: Quality that is recognised nationally in terms of originality, significance and rigour.
- Unclassified: Quality that falls below the standard of nationally recognised work. Or work which does not meet the published definition of research for the purposes of this assessment.

The reader may note the high level of quality expected here. One could write an article focused on English child welfare, which is original, significant and rigorous and the outcome would be that this is a 'one star' article, as it is focused on England – a high hurdle indeed. This provides another example of how audits and metrics have an impact on everyday practice: they can be distressing and demotivating. Like all the issues discussed in this book, the process is potentially subject to game playing. As an example of this a colleague of mine once advised people planning submission of journal articles to use phrases such as 'internationally relevant' and 'globally resonant' to potentially push the article up the star ratings – even though the substance of the article would be largely the same. As Collini acidly comments:

> The fashion for slapping the adjective 'global' in front of a wide variety of nouns often simply indicates a mixture of slackness and hype. (2012: 13)

Before the regulations were changed it was also possible, under the previous RAE (Research Assessment Exercise) regime, to entice researchers and their teams from one university to another, in order to boost the receiving universities scores. Clearly, this benefited the receiving universities but it is difficult to see how this boosts the quality of the national body of research.

One of the respondents felt rather alienated from the entire process, reflecting on how the process works better for the identified elite universities:

> I would say like it is an event rather than a process – it is difficult in a non-research-intensive university – it is hard to fully engage. It doesn't apply to me – there is a narrow focus on what counts as research. I find it disappointing that pedagogical research does not get the same weight as say industrial-based research. It is disappointing that there isn't more focus on what we actually do: it doesn't reflect what we are about. (Respondent One)

The academic Derek Sayer has made a trenchant critique of the REF (Sayer 2015b). In a related article in *The Guardian* newspaper Sayer (2105a) makes five key points which are explained and summarised here.

First, Sayer argues that the REF costs too much. He points out that for the 2014 exercise over 1,000 academic panel members spent their time giving a score to 191,232 outputs. To get to this point, individual academics, university leaders and administrators spent hours preparing for the REF, undertaking mock exercises and engaging external consultants to advise on the process. Sayer reports that the cost was around £47 million of university money and £12 million in HEFCE (Higher Education Funding Council for England) administrative costs. My guess would be that preparation for the 2021 exercise (delayed by COVID-19) significantly outstrips this – with a more complex REF and with an extended preparation time. Sayer's argument about cost resonates with the points made elsewhere in this book in relation to audit and measurement regimes more generally.

Second, Sayer argues that the REF purports to be peer review, but actually it is not. In his book, Sayer (2015b) argues this point extensively and persuasively. Peer review is a complex and detailed process undertaken before journal articles can be published. Usually peer review is undertaken by two scholars, or perhaps by up to six, and often drawing on an international pool of high status academics: it is a double-blind process where the names of the authors and referees are unknown to the other party. In contrast the REF panels are almost exclusively from British universities, the authors are identifiable and, as Sayer reports, one reviewer may be asked to review over 1,000 papers, whilst also undertaking their full-time job.

Third, Sayer argues that the REF process undermines collegiality. The process has changed over the years, but for the 2014 exercise Sayer is referring to the process of selecting staff to be included in the REF, which his book covers in detail. He argues that this was devastating for staff morale and a sense of collectivity in university departments. The process is more inclusive in 2021 but puts considerable pressure on colleagues with large teaching and administrative roles to also be active researchers. This process also creates a dichotomy between high status, international profile researchers and lower status, lower profile but extremely hard-working teaching staff. A theme of this book is that the audit culture undermines co-operation and generates competition.

Sayer's fourth point is that the REF process discourages innovation. This point is well illustrated by Professor Donald Braben who argues that the work of Crick and Watson on DNA, Brenner on molecular biology, Peter D. Mitchell on the chemiosmotic process and Perutz and Kendrew on haemoglobin structure would not have 'survived the current REF regime' (UCU, n.d.).

Sayer's fifth, and final, point is that the REF is redundant as it tells us what will already be known from other forms of data collection.

I would add my own critique to that of Sayer: it is about the crude reductionism of the process. To provide an example, one of my own personal favourite books, thankfully produced before the REF process, is E.P. Thompson's *The Making of the English Working Class* (1963). The work is a majestic survey of social and industrial change in England drawing on a wide range of sources. The thought of a panel debating whether this is a 1*, a 2*, a 3* or a 4* is really quite bizarre. One may argue that, in retrospect, it does not fully cover issues relating to women or children, and some may wish to argue that due to its focus on England it is indeed 1*. Such a debate is an extreme example of reductionism – quite literally reducing almost 1,000 pages to a single digit (I am not sure of the role of the star as even 1 seems to merit a star).

I am not qualified to comment on the grading processes in the natural sciences – but certainly in the social sciences there are paradigm wars that make it hard to evaluate the work of colleagues. In sociology we have feminist scholars, critical race theorists and post-modernists to mention just a few. It would be very difficult to envisage a social scientist committed to statistical approaches, for example, being able to reach a judgement on an abstract piece of queer theory. There is quite simply no universal judgement of quality, certainly not in the social sciences.

To provide an example, drawing on my primary field of social work, some scholars are highly committed to Randomised Controlled Trials (RCTs) whereas others regard these as unethical in certain circumstances. The importance of this is demonstrated by a debate about the appropriateness of RCTs in the context of a process called Family Group Conferences (FGCs). A research centre known as the What Works Centre outlined a study of FGCs using a RCT methodology. In turn, a group of academics challenged the ethics of the project and argued that 'some families will be denied the opportunity to exercise their rights and responsibilities in order to produce evidence for professionals and policy makers' and pointed out that 'this is markedly different to experiencing uneven access to FGC services across the UK, instead this is curtailing the opportunity to exercise rights in the name of evidence' (Turner 2019). The What Works Centre strongly defended the project: 'Conducting research badly, coming to the end and not learning the answers to questions, that would be unethical' (Turner 2019). This issue illustrates the arguments in this study: how can one side of this argument, regardless of the merits of each side, allocate a starred judgement to an article by the 'other side', and this in any way be regarded as 'objective'.

In addition to the submission of books and articles, universities are also asked to submit impact case studies – something that carries a weighting of 25% in the 2021 exercise, compared to 60% allocated for outputs and 15% for the research environment. The case studies are to 'assess the "reach and significance" of impacts on the economy, society, culture, public policy or services, health, the environment or quality of life' (REF2021 2020: 7). I felt sympathetic to impact case studies in my field (of social work) as it seems to value work that made a difference rather than publishing work in obscure journals read by few. Derek Sayer is concerned that this is actually about economic impact and utility and will discourage blue skies and other forms of innovative research. I have produced two of these impact statements during my career. The last one I wrote was honest, accurate and written as a fair account of my impact, trying to avoid exaggeration and over-assessment of impact: the feedback from an external assessor was that I 'clearly did not understand the process' and the statement would have to be rewritten, by someone other than myself, in order to assess impact more accurately. Clearly, I did not understand how to play the game required by the REF, even though I provided a fair and balanced account.

Barnett and Moher use a sophisticated methodology to construct an alternative research league table based on more socially relevant, ethical criteria and conclude:

> Current league tables place a high value on the quantity of research outputs and citations … It is hard to imagine why most universities continue to support the current ranking schemes given that they may be reducing the positive value universities have on society. We believe there is merit in considering alternative more socially responsible criteria for ranking universities. (Barnett and Moher 2019)

Collini summarises the issue around the research audits as follows:

> What can be said is that the RAE is a crude form of measurement that is used to distribute funds to universities: its indisputable effect has been to encourage academics to publish more, and more quickly. It is not obvious, let alone indisputable, that this situation has been conducive to any 'increase in quality'. (2012: 160)

TEACHING EXCELLENCE FRAMEWORK

Following the introduction of the RAE/REF system there developed a critique that this undervalued teaching, as this was not subject to a comparable exercise. Partly as a result of this and as a part of the audit explosion more generally the Teaching Excellence Framework (TEF) was introduced with the first exercise being undertaken in 2016–17. The process is described as follows by Neary:

> Excellence is to be measured through a series of proxy metrics that include, student satisfaction, retention, employability and a new metric, learning gain, which sets out to record the improvement in knowledge and personal development of students during their time in higher education. (2016: 690)

There are various critiques of the system that generates an award of Gold, Silver or Bronze to each university. As could be predicted Oxford and Cambridge, for example, gained the Gold award. There was, however, one noteworthy outlier – the London School of Economics was granted a bronze award putting them alongside Kingston Maurward College and the Northern College of Acupuncture, for example. In their original submission LSE are defensive, arguing that their lower than expected NSS scores reflect a London-factor, which is that the high cost of living in London makes students less satisfied. Interesting in the context of the arguments in this book, in their submission LSE argue that:

> LSE's performance in the core metrics is a partial – and not entirely accurate – reflection of the education that our students experience at the School. (Office for Students 2016).

The LSE website contains a reflection by Jessica Patterson (2015) who argues that the TEF is dysfunctional on the following grounds:

1. The system is already broken – referring to the REF as a doubtful role model.

2. The TEF is designed as a system for introducing higher fees for higher scorers.

3. The link between a high TEF score and graduate careers is a simplistic measure of quality.

4. Metrics can be used negatively to discipline lecturers.

5. The TEF creates an unfairly stratified HE system.

Further, a study drawing on the views of almost 6,000 higher education staff argues that:

> Our findings raise fundamental concerns, methodologically and conceptually, about the fitness for the purpose of the TEF and its failure to take into account the views and experiences of higher education staff. With a reliance on proxy metrics that emphasise the economic value of higher education over the quality of teaching, we explore how the TEF lacks legitimacy and credibility as an instrument of measurement of teaching excellence across all levels of the workforce. We also argue that the processes informing the TEF fail to take into account the experiences and perceptions of staff directly involved in teaching, which given their centrality to the quality and development of higher education, seems a lamentable exclusion. (Cui, French and O'Leary 2019: 1)

Frankham adds to this critique as follows:

> I argue that students' focus on outcomes (which at face value suggests they have internalized the importance of employment) is contributing to the production of graduates who do not have the dispositions that employers – when interviewed – say that they want. The highly performative culture of higher education, encouraged by the same metrics that will be extended through the TEF, is implicated then in not preparing students for the workplace. (2017: 628)

My respondents reflect this general disenchantment and disengagement with the TEF:

> I have only been peripheral to [the TEF] – it is very narrow about what constitutes learning and teaching. What I feel from where I have been involved – they're blunt measures. The narrative is not sufficient to contextualise the blunt instruments. There is no real measure of how you add value – particularly for a uni that is widening participation and addressing civic responsibilities – it is just not captured. Attendance, retention, hours, degrees doesn't tell the whole story about higher education and its transformational potential in deprived areas. It is all geared to traditional unis – it focuses on the 'sausage machine' Russell group university approach. It has a high profile, it is seen as really important, due to the reputation factor and the marketing. It feels like the TEF is an exercise to do when the TEF is due … it should be embedded and not seen as an end in itself. It becomes the iron cage of bureaucracy – you complete something to meet a requirement. It is a bureaucratic requirement rather than a means of QA. (Respondent One)

The other respondent notes that:

> people in general knew the parameters, but it was phenomenally complicated in terms of the statistical returns. It was meant to highlight what goes on in the classrooms but because of the metrics it became vastly complicated. So what was required internally was for the exercise to be strongly centrally run with not a great deal of engagement by teaching staff. The TEF was calculated in advance given our past record – we knew the most we could get was bronze. We knew the outcome before we did the actual exercise, it was weird. (Respondent Two)

Thus, we seem to end up with yet another metric, which alienates staff and which provides questionable judgements – whilst costing a considerable amount of money and staff time.

CONCLUSION

The sum of the audit approach to universities is that it reflects a meritocracy – the best and most mobile students can study the league table and select the best universities and the bulk of the research money goes to the universities with the highest scores in the REF: it is a self-reproducing meritocracy. Rowan Moore explains how gaming and metrics help to reproduce a meritocracy:

> The gaming of metrics also favours those institutions with the business nous and the resources to do it better than others, which tends to mean those that are

already larger and more successful. Which contributes to another deficiency of the imperfect market in higher education – that it favours not necessarily those offering the best and most valuable courses, but those best equipped to operate the strange machinery of incentives and opportunities. (Moore 2021)

Michael Sandel has produced an excellent critique of meritocracy in his book *The Tyranny of Merit* (2020): his focus is on individual meritocracy and credentialism, but is transferable to our more institutional discussion. Sandel argues that meritocracy reinforces existing inequalities and ignores that there is not a level playing field. He argues that pure luck is a factor that is often under-played and that meritocracy undermines importance differences – for example, that hospital cleaners who are essential to successful societies are not well awarded by meritocratic systems. A similar argument applies to universities – there are existing systems that simply award pre-existing merit. Oxford and Cambridge have the highest income, the highest entrance tariffs, come top of league tables and therefore attract more high-achieving students and then the system reproduces itself. One of the respondents agreed about the role of league tables:

> Again they're difficult, they're not accurate and they're blunt instruments – they reflect a didactic model of education. A couple of the new universities have broken the mould, ones that are not Russell group, but you see the hierarchy of Russell group, red brick universities, it is skewed towards the traditional model. It perpetuates the elitist model of higher education. (Respondent One)

I conclude with an anecdote – hopefully an illustrative one. I worked at a university which used a number of Key Performance Indicators (KPIs). One such indicator was the number of registered PhD students for each faculty. The result was that the elation of a successful PhD viva was rather diluted by the fact that the success of the student meant that your faculty's performance had declined as the number of registered PhD students had fallen from, say, 32 to 31. This illustrates the banality of metrics and a paradox common to the misuse of statistical measures.

3

TARGETS AND TRANSPARENCY IN THE NHS: PROMOTING PATIENT CHOICE THROUGH THE AUDIT CULTURE

The second case study in this book concerns the National Health Service (NHS) in the United Kingdom. Arguably the NHS is the public institution closest to the hearts and minds of the British public, held to be a model for much of the rest of the world: it is therefore profoundly political, with all the political parties hoping to be positioned as the guardians of the NHS. The NHS also costs more than any other form of publicly funded service in the United Kingdom (HM Treasury 2020). The cost and the issue of political contestation raises issues of transparency and accountability which are often high profile and controversial: are waiting lists longer than they were? What are the waiting times for accident and emergency cases? Is one hospital trust more efficient than another? Is one consultant more effective than another? As Muller states:

> Nowhere are metrics in greater vogue than in the field of medicine. Nowhere, perhaps, are they more promising. And the stakes are high. (2018: 105)

In order to assess these and many other audit issues, the role of the Care Quality Commission, targets and league tables, consultant performance will be explored and critically analysed. As with the other case studies, experienced professionals were interviewed: in this case two experienced senior nurses were interviewed together and agreed with each other's comments so are included as Respondent Three: Respondent Four is an experienced senior consultant working within the NHS.

LEAGUE TABLES AND GAMING SYSTEMS

The NHS is a universal service, importantly free at the point of use (although it is difficult to understand why optical services and dental care are excluded from this mantra). The original aim of the service in the National Health Service Act 1946 was to provide an equal service across the country, where people could access care locally:

1. It shall be the duty of the Minister of Health (hereafter in this Act referred to as 'the Minister') to promote the establishment in England and Wales of a comprehensive health service designed to secure improvement in the physical and mental health of the people of England and Wales and the prevention, diagnosis and treatment of illness, and for that purpose to provide or secure the effective provision of services in accordance with the following provisions of this Act.

2. The services so provided shall be free of charge, except where any provision of this Act expressly provides for the making and recovery of charges.

This original vision seems to be of a national service, which would be similar throughout the United Kingdom. The contemporary NHS Constitution states this principle as follows:

> It is available to all irrespective of gender, race, disability, age, sexual orientation, religion, belief, gender reassignment, pregnancy and maternity or marital or civil partnership status. The service is designed to improve, prevent, diagnose and treat both physical and mental health problems with equal regard. It has a duty to each and every individual that it serves and must respect their human rights. At the same time, it has a wider social duty to promote equality through the services it provides and to pay particular attention to groups or sections of society where improvements in health and life expectancy are not keeping pace with the rest of the population. (NHS Constitution for England: DH&SC, updated 2021)

Regardless of this, across the decades, it has become apparent that equal access to health services is a complex challenge and the NHS has been unable to address inequalities in health outcomes. Morris and colleagues, for example, carried out a study in relation to inequality of access to health:

> We investigate inequality and inequity in the use of GPs, outpatient visits, day cases and in-patient stays with a unique linked data set which combines rich recent information on the subjective and objective health of individuals and

their socio-economic circumstances with information on local supply condi-
tions. After controlling for need variables such as age, sex, health and for the
supply of health care, we find that utilisation is linked to income, ethnicity, economic status and education. Low-income individuals and ethnic minorities have
lower use of secondary care despite having higher use of primary care. (Morris,
Sutton and Gravelle 2005: 1251)

There is clearly an issue with equality of access to health, which has been
explored most pre-eminently by Sir Michael Marmot and his team (2020). One
response to these access and equality issues has been to introduce choice into
the system, as championed by Tony Blair as Prime Minister (1997–2008) and
his various Secretaries of State for Health:

> Patients are being offered direct choices over the hospital at which they will
> receive their treatment. From December 2005, patients referred for 'elective'
> [non-emergency] surgery will be able to choose from four or five providers.
> From 2008, choice will be unlimited as long as the provider meets NHS stand-
> ards and can deliver at the NHS price. (King's Fund 2005: 10)

All the public institutions explored in this book have been subject to some form
of marketisation and competition. This relates to the main themes of this book
as marketisation requires data, claims of transparency, ratings, procurement
and accounting methods. The market does not exist spontaneously in the public services, it has to be constructed and created by a series of policy decisions,
for example:

> In addition to these structural changes, the Government is also implementing
> a new method of allocating resources within the NHS, known as 'payment by
> results'. Under this system, there is a national tariff [prices] for operations and
> procedures, and hospitals will receive a set price for the care they provide to
> each patient. (King's Fund 2005: 10)

There exists a complex dynamic between the work of health professionals,
health inequalities and accountability. One issue with the audit culture is holding professionals accountable for issues beyond their control. Muller reflects
upon this issue, in the US context as follows:

> Many of the problems of American health are a function not of the medical sys-
> tem but of social and cultural factors beyond the medical system. (2018: 106)

Poor health outcomes are generated by social inequalities, the food and
tobacco industry and air pollution, for example, issues beyond the immediate

reach of health care professionals. It is perhaps partly due to these wider factors that the audit culture seems to change little in terms of quality:

> what is quite astonishing is how often these techniques ... have no discernible effect on outcomes. (Muller 2018: 115)

This chapter goes on to explore the mobilisation of the audit culture within the NHS and how the search for measurement has helped to shape the experience of both patients and professionals.

DOCTORS AND LEAGUE TABLES

The construction of choice in the NHS has been a complex and demanding route. Choice assumes the existence of the rational consumer – a person who can make the best choice, from a range of goods or services, drawing on reliable information. Even in competitive market situations this scenario is demanding of the consumer, and has a mythical quality. If a person is buying a car, for example, it is unlikely that any one of us can fully compute the differences between makes, reliability, warranties, performance, road tax variation and so on. In reality we are perhaps persuaded by a convenient garage or website and an attractive colour. As we shall see, comparing hospitals, or surgeons, is an even more complex exercise and assumes we have the time, expertise and necessary access to technology to make an informed choice. Locality and ease of access is probably the major driver, especially if we are going to be in hospital for some time and expecting visitors.

The decline of trust, the illusion of choice and the measurement of everything have led, for example, to the creation of league tables for consultants. The initial data publication was promoted by both professionals and politicians in the name of transparency. Nursing Times reported the launch of the MyNHS website, in 2014, as follows:

> NHS England's medical director Professor Sir Bruce Keogh who has championed transparency in the NHS, said the website will drive up standards. 'This represents another major step forward on the transparency journey', he said. 'It will help drive up standards, and we are committed to expanding publication into other areas. The results demonstrate that surgery in this country is as good as anywhere in the western world and, in some specialities, it is better ... The surgical community in this country deserves a great deal of credit for being a world leader in this area.' (*Nursing Times* 2014)

This drive for transparency was supported politically by the then Secretary of State for Health, Jeremy Hunt, who added that:

Transparency is about patient outcomes, not process targets. It uses the power of a learning culture and of peer review, not blame. Healthcare globally has been slow to develop the kind of safety culture based on openness and transparency that has become normal in the airline, oil and nuclear industries … The NHS is now blazing a trail across the world as the first major health economy to adopt this kind of culture. (*Nursing Times* 2014)

This data was launched in a blaze of publicity and hyperbole, it was to be available on the MyNHS website, but despite the high profile launch the project was short-lived. When we log on to this site today we are met with the following announcement:

The MyNHS website has closed. Why MyNHS is closing

The MyNHS site is not used enough to justify the costs of running it. The NHS is committed to delivering value for money and has therefore decided to close the site.

Transparency and openness about how data is used to improve the health and care system remains a priority. NHSX, NHS England and NHS Digital will continue to work together to understand how we can achieve this. (www.nhs.uk/mynhs/index.html)

Given the closure of this website I have done my best to locate existing data and league tables, understand these and report on them – but I have found it an onerous and largely thankless task. Exactly how this data would help, say, an 80-year-old woman wanting a knee replacement who did not have access to a computer remains a mystery. I report below the outcomes of many hours of largely fruitless labour. I randomly chose the example of knee replacement surgery. The data is reported as it appears on https://surgeonprofile.njrcentre.org.uk/SurgeonListing.

In the case of my randomly selected knee replacement surgeon I found this data difficult to dissect and understand. For example, if I was going to have a knee replacement the last thing I would worry about would be dying but this is covered in the data as follows:

This shows 90-day mortality following knee surgery for this surgeon, based on the type of patients this surgeon has seen.

The surgeon you are reviewing is highlighted as an orange triangle. Progression along the horizontal axis (x axis) means that the surgeon has done more cases and/or cases at a higher mortality risk such as older patients. Progression along the vertical axis (y axis) means the surgeon has had more deaths.

The vertical axis figures are presented as a standardised mortality ratio. This means the values do not represent percentages of patients who have died, but they represent the proportion of deaths compared to the national average. The data is also risk adjusted to take account of the fact that different surgeons may operate on more higher-risk or lower-risk patients e.g. because of demographics in the patient population they work with.

- Surgeons on the central (green) horizontal line (at national average ratio figure of 1) have had exactly the average expected mortality
- Surgeons either side of the central green line but below the upper red line have had a level of mortality that is within the expected range
- Any surgeons that appear above the top red line which represents a Control limit (99.8%) have a mortality rate that is higher than expected.

The overall 90-day mortality rate following primary knee replacement surgery is approximately 0.2%. (https://surgeonprofile.njrcentre.org.uk/SurgeonListing)

This data then is difficult to understand and analyse: certainly beyond my expertise. For each surgeon there is also a 12 and 36 month Practice Profile: I explored my selected surgeon and the figures suggested that the particular surgeon is operating systematically below the national average in terms of the operations performed. This may well be a positive and could show that the surgeon is selective in the work they undertake: they are not over-pressured, nor junior and inexperienced, and are perhaps able to control their workload. But it may also be negative because it could also show that they are relatively inexperienced compared with others and perhaps not chosen by many people. The explanation provided in a note on Operation Sub-category is extremely complicated and it is far from clear how it maps onto the categories in the table. For the randomly selected surgeon the 90-day mortality rate for hip replacements is below the national average, which we can regard as positive, but is simultaneously low in the scale of cases with a high-mortality risk. This fits with the data in the table on the patients who were treated, but does it mean that maybe the surgeon is risk averse in the selection of patients, or maybe not considered safe with the more difficult cases? If as a patient I am a bit overweight and I have not been well, I may ask will I be safe? For this same surgeon the 90-day mortality for knees is potentially more concerning: the surgeon does not do many high-risk cases compared with the national average, but his mortality rate is higher than the national average. Presented in the tables is a red line which states that anyone below it is below the expected rate. But if a surgeon comes anywhere near the line, what exactly does this mean and how should this be interpreted? This data took me some hours to comprehend. I asked a colleague with statistical expertise to look at the surgeon's profile and they commented as follows:

These figures are as likely to mislead as they are to reassure and they pre-suppose quite a high degree of statistical sophistication as well as some background knowledge of how hospitals work. So the question has to be asked when compiling this data: what is the least knowledgeable patient likely to infer? Probably the answer to that is that they would not even look at the tables: but there is a lot of scope for misunderstanding. I do not understand the mortality tables myself. I get the general idea but what the control limit is and why it's 99.8% I have no idea. And what on earth is the use of the Orthopaedic Data Evaluation Panel-rated implant table?

An article published in the *British Medical Journal* agrees with the issues about the interpretation of data and the complexity involved in this:

> NHS performance league tables are difficult to comprehend and easy to misinterpret, but their publication by an official body lends them credence. (Adab, Rouse, Mohammed and Marshall 2002: 97)

As previously stated, it seems strange that the data on knee replacement places such a strong emphasis on mortality rates following knee surgery. The figure that needs to be highlighted here is that overall mortality is 0.2% – which seems to be a low figure and one would want to know if these deaths were closely related to the operation or to other external factors? Thus you seem to have a performance table that highlights death-rate, but death is hardly the most significant outcome in this context and seems alarmist. What patients facing this kind of surgery need to know is how successful the operation will be in terms of relieving pain or whether further operations will be needed and if this varies between surgeons?

My statistician colleague concludes as follows:

> This is all data that might be useful for medical reviewers, but overall a better purpose would be served by the hospital having a general statement about how orthopaedic surgeons are quality-assessed, just to provide reassurance. Throwing this kind of data onto a prospective patient is putting a burden on them that is not properly theirs to carry.

The professional community itself seems to be divided on the publication of such data. Critics say the data is "crude" and can be misleading as it does not include essential information such as duration of hospital stay and returns to theatre (National Health Executive 2014).

Adab and colleagues provide a critique of league tables as follows:

Firstly, the value of any performance indicator depends on the quality of the data used in its calculation. Unfortunately, many NHS data have been of poor quality, partly because the NHS relies on the co-operation of health service providers and depends on their data management systems. Another justified criticism is that not all outcomes valued by society are measurable, and most NHS performance indicators have been selected on the basis of what is available and practical rather than what is meaningful. (2002: 96)

Consistent with the arguments of this book, and the earlier point about the myth of the rational consumer, Adab and colleagues point out that:

Performance league tables may also improve patients' choice, and proponents argue that this is necessary for an efficient market economy by encouraging consumers to seek out high ranking providers. This is largely irrelevant in Britain, however, as patients have little choice when they use the services of a doctor, clinic, or hospital. Furthermore, a systematic review of the literature on the effects of public release of performance data showed that individual consumers and purchasers don't search out, understand, or use available data. (2002: 97)

Magee and colleagues undertook focus groups with 50 participants about choice and how it was influenced by data and conclude that:

Participants felt that independent monitoring of healthcare performance is necessary, but they were ambivalent about the value of performance indicators and hospital rankings. They tended to distrust government information and preferred the presentational style of 'Dr Foster', a commercial information provider, because it gave more detailed locally relevant information. Many participants felt the NHS did not offer much scope for choice of provider. If public access to performance information is to succeed in informing referral decisions and raising quality standards, the public and general practitioners will need education on how to interpret and use the data. (Magee, Davis and Coulter 2003: 338)

In our case studies examining schools (Chapter 4) and children's social care (Chapter 5) we argue that identifying so-called poor performers can be an unfair process, a point also made by Adab and colleagues in the health context:

Unfortunately, with ranking of performance, there is an implicit assumption that providers located towards the bottom provide a worse service .... apportioning of blame is generally unfair as it ignores the fact that modern medicine is a complex process …. Providers with poor performance scores inevitably argue that they treat patients with more complex problems and that insufficient adjustment has been made for their case mix. Indeed, small differences in patients' age, sex, medical history, and social class can change performance indicator scores and a provider's relative position in a league table. (2002: 97)

The latter points also apply to university league tables (Chapter 2 of this book) where numerical scores can be fairly similar, but places in the league tables can vary significantly. The point about complexity and how metrics tend to reduce complex situations to figures is another recurring theme of this book and can also lead to practice that is about improving metrics rather than about improving quality:

> Unintended consequences are high on the list of criticisms of pay for performance and the risks of perverse or unintended consequences associated with the publication of performance data are well known. Pay-for-performance programs can reward only what can be measured and attributed, a limitation that can lead to less holistic care and inappropriate concentration of the doctor's gaze on what can be measured rather than on what is important. (Hamel, Roland and Campbell 2014: 1947)

Adab and colleagues also make a point about gaming, reflecting Muller's point discussed in Chapter 1, exploring the issue of playing the system in order to get the best possible results:

> Unfortunately, there is little agreement among experts on the validity of various strategies for risk adjustment. As a result, some argue that, in order to avoid a poor ranking, providers may refuse to treat critically ill patients or may refer them to other hospitals. (Adab et al. 2002: 97)

Adab and colleagues conclude their argument as follows, reflecting my attempt at understanding the data:

> NHS performance league tables are difficult to comprehend and easy to misinterpret, but their publication by an official body lends them credence. (2002: 97)

One of the respondents interviewed for this study felt all the bureaucracy behind the league tables was unnecessary as data was always gathered in any case:

We gathered our own audit data in relation to the number of complications and successes, so we did not really need the centrally gathered data. We collected the data on ourselves. (Respondent Four)

In terms of targets, which were predominant in New Labour era, this respondent describes the impact of the target culture:

[in relation to targets] it was the pressure of work that was put on us in case people went over their date that really had an impact. There was a last minute rush to get people done even over the weekend as they had to get people done by, say, the Monday. As a result the emergency cases were ignored by management but they would pay extra money to make sure someone didn't go over the 18 week target. (Respondent Four)

The targets then become an administrative, rather than a medical driven process:

The people putting the operating list were administrators – not consultants, we have lost control of it. It wasn't based on clinical need but more based on are they going to run out of time, according to the targets. (Respondent Four)

Mike Power notes this as a significant development in the relationship between professionalism and the audit culture:

Tensions are revealed in the form of hierarchical struggles between medical practitioners and emergent managers over the control of the evaluation process. (1997: 105)

O'Neill makes a similar point:

Doctors speak of the inroads that required record-keeping makes into the time that they can spend finding out what is wrong with their patients and listening to their patients. (2002: 50)

The most notorious target in the English context was one whereby every patient should be seen within four hours of arrival in Accident and Emergency. Muller comments that:

The program succeeded – at least on the surface. In fact, some hospitals responded by keeping incoming patients in queues of ambulances, beyond the doors of the hospital, until the staff was confident that the patient could be seen within the allotted four hours to be admitted. (2018: 5)

This provides a powerful example of the dysfunction and unintended consequences that can arise from targets and related aspects of an audit culture reflecting the displacement of trust, the creation of unnecessary bureaucracy and dangers of gaming.

THE INSPECTION PROCESS AND THE CARE QUALITY COMMISSION

Services provided by the NHS (plus other services such as care homes and private hospitals) are inspected by the Care Quality Commission (CQC from here on). The aim of the CQC is described on their website (www.cqc.org.uk) as follows:

> We make sure health and social care services provide people with safe, effective, compassionate, high-quality care and we encourage care services to improve.

These reports are published on the CQC website and are easily accessible and readable.

The CQC inspection reports provide a traffic light system addressing the following questions:

Are services safe?

Are services effective?

Are services caring?

Are services responsive?

Are services well led?

Are resources used productively?

The inspection process based on these key questions leads to an inspection report, which includes a rating (using the same wording as Ofsted): inadequate, requires improvement, good or outstanding.

My respondents in the health service were generally more positive about the inspection process than those in the education and children's social care field and provide a balanced and nuanced account of their experiences. The two senior nurses interviewed explained their role as follows:

> We hold strategic roles and we lead the process. We provide a lot of guidance and support to the providers. (Respondent Three)

The dominance of the inspection process and the apprehension that it brings is a recurring theme for many of our respondents throughout this study:

> Inspection is a very intense experience. I have always said when the e-mail arrives everything stops and diaries are cleared of everything else. All we do (after this) is preparation for the inspection. It is nerve-wracking and everything stops for inspection preparation. (Respondent Three)

There is an additional complication for the NHS, that of multiple over-lapping providers and frequent inspections:

> The complexity is interesting and challenging: if there are multiple providers it is really complex to co-ordinate. I don't think that the complexity is really understood by the CQC. The rhythm varies – I would say normally about one inspection every 18 months, but recently I think we had about four within a 12 month period. (Respondent Three)

The preparation process for these intense inspection processes is very demanding:

> Gathering the required data for a Single Inspection Framework was interesting and very challenging ... For a recent multi-agency Joint Targeted Area Inspection we were required to undertake seven multi-agency audits before the inspection even started. How to lead an inspection? We have learnt about that. We have draft letters and loads of stuff ready to go. Whether it makes a difference to children is hard to see. (Respondent Three)

The respondents note the variability of inspection according to who the Lead Inspector is – a theme developed by both our children's social care and school-based respondents:

> In relation to the CQC the approach to the inspection is very much down to the Lead Inspector. Inspectors are variable, some are outstanding, they seem authentic and create a good dialogue ... One inspector said inappropriate things that revealed a lack of experience. It is very variable, some inspectors just don't understand the issues. (Respondent Three)

Whilst the health-based respondents were generally more positive about the inspection process than our school and social care respondents – they did have some challenging experiences, referring to a recent inspection as 'evil'. They continue:

> The staff see inspectors as God. More than once we have spent time mopping up staff who felt unfairly criticised and often the criticism was inappropriate. (Respondent Three)

The process of feedback and the resultant outcomes are challenging:

> The bad news is often in the written report with the verbal feedback seeming more positive. You struggle to see positive outcomes from the inspection process – but you can pull out some examples. …, one or two have helped us, but often we were already on with them. I am not sure that the positive outcomes equals the effort that we put in. (Respondent Three)

Outcomes can also be traumatic as in the following example:

> CQC walked in and inspected our sexual assault centre and they closed it two days later. Not due to the service but due to the physical environment … you can imagine the absolute chaos. (Respondent Three)

The two senior nurses had significant experience of preparing for inspections, and also for implementing recommendations. They felt that there was some learning but that:

> The downside is that some recommendations absolutely are not SMART [specific, measurable, achievable, realistic and time-bounded] – they are often unachievable. You put a lot of effort into delivering them but they were not well written. Some are unachievable. (Respondent Three)

This point resonates with one made by Mike Power:

> The value of medical auditing becomes harder to demonstrate the more it is disengaged from local learning processes. It is rather a practice that must be made to work. (1997: 109)

These senior nurses had experience of joint inspections and could contrast the impact of CQC inspections (discussed in Chapter 5) with Ofsted-led processes:

> In some providers there can be very, very challenging inspections and the Chief Executive and the Chief Nurses have moved on. The CQC inspections are slicker and less traumatic than the ones led by Ofsted. (Respondent Three)

The respondents noted the level of anxiety in the local authority sector:

> If the local authority has a bad inspection then it follows that heads will roll, someone will have to bite the bullet. The focus is on over-presenting and even on different versions of the truth. If you are asked to be part of a focus group and you know some of the information is not correct. The fear of leaders losing their jobs is a reality in some areas. We have been kept out of focus groups as

we may say things that politically are not welcomed. Inspections should only be one part of the barometer. (Respondent Three)

They found the inspections of service for children looked after (CLA) were more positive as they were narrative based rather than summary judgements:

The CLA inspections are not simply judgements any more, a narrative is much more helpful. (Respondent Three)

This again suggests that the complexity of service provision is best addressed by a narrative rather than by reductive single, or two word, judgements. The respondents had ideas in terms of how the system could be improved, suggesting that peer review may well be a helpful process:

If we had the time and developed the expertise the peer review can be much more helpful. (Respondent Three)

They would like more time to develop a quality service using the data that is available and by involving service users more comprehensively:

You get all the data but there isn't time to triangulate say by doing a ward visit and ask if for example the ward staff know how to do a child protection referral. In an ideal world we would involve parents and children, they could be involved more. If we spoke more to the child you could triangulate information better, which would support and drive up practice. (Respondent Three)

It is also hard for them to spot consistency in the current inspection regimes and more continuity would be welcome:

It is difficult to compare one inspection to another, the regime changes ... they are like oranges and lemons. (Respondent Three)

The inspection system within the NHS seems to have both strengths and weaknesses: whilst producing some helpful development comments it also shares many of the weaknesses and challenges explored in the other case studies in this book.

One of the narratives shared by our respondents is that audit culture imposes a bureaucratic burden on professionals who would rather be getting on with their work with service users. Respondent Four, a retired senior consultant, reflected on the relationship between medicine, professionalism and bureaucracy. He was a defender of high standards, professionalism and accountability but felt that the system of maintaining professional registration had gone too far:

> [in relation to professional accreditation] it was not necessary, it was a waste of time and of money going on repetitive courses that didn't tell you anything. It took up a lot of time and you didn't learn anything new at all. It all cost a lot of money: the hospital needs to know people are keeping up-to-date but it all went much too far. In total it was 10 to 12 days away [from practice]. (Respondent Four)

This applied to the professional appraisal system as well:

> For the annual appraisal we had to demonstrate that we had been on courses relevant to our practice. A peer, that is another consultant, undertook the appraisal, but it was like doing your driving test time and time again. (Respondent Four)

There were also advantages to this system recognised by this respondent:

> You did learn through the appraisal system, we were getting feedback from patients and this was useful. (Respondent Four)

CONCLUSION

The audit culture is dominant in health care: a dominance closely related to the promotion of choice and competition within the system. We have seen that the data relating to consultants' performance is complex, hard to understand and not always easily accessible: whilst no doubt useful to analysts and researchers it is hard to perceive how this is useful in the promotion of patient choice. The target culture has also had some unintended consequences, including some game playing and the notorious allegations of ambulances waiting outside Accident and Emergency so as not to start the four-hour wait clock ticking. Our health care respondents are more positive about the inspection system than our social work and teacher respondents, whilst also expressing some well-reasoned reservations.

4

SCHOOLS AND THE ROLE OF OFSTED: 'YOU COULD HEAR THE SOUND OF STAPLE GUNS IN THE CORRIDORS DAWN TO DUSK!'

The inspection, grading and the production of league tables in relation to schooling has become the highest public profile of all the inspection, grading and metrics systems. Schools often have banners proclaiming their positive Ofsted outcomes to the passing public, estate agents now routinely report on the grading of local schools and this in turn is said to have an impact on house prices in the locality of highly graded schools (Machin 2011). This chapter explores the powerful role of the audit culture within schooling and the issues and challenges arising from this. As in the other case studies, two experienced professionals were interviewed to inform the analysis of the data sources and inspection processes explored here.

THE INSPECTION PROCESS

Ofsted – originally the Office for Standards in Education (now with Children's Services and Skills appended) – was founded in 1992, absorbing the role of Her Majesty's Inspectors, who first came into being in 1839. Ofsted report their function as follows:

> Ofsted's role is to make sure that organisations providing education, training and care services in England do so to a high standard for children and students.
>
> Every week, we carry out hundreds of inspections and regulatory visits throughout England and publish the results online.

We report directly to Parliament and we are independent and impartial. (www.gov.uk/government/organisations/ofsted/about)

They describe their responsibilities and priorities as follows:

We're responsible for:

Inspecting

- maintained schools and academies, some independent schools, and many other educational institutions and programmes outside of higher education
- childcare, adoption and fostering agencies and initial teacher training

Regulating

- a range of early years and children's social care services, making sure they're suitable for children and potentially vulnerable young people

Reporting

- publishing reports of our findings so they can be used to improve the overall quality of education and training
- informing policymakers about the effectiveness of these services

Our priorities

We will ensure that:

- all of our work is evidence-led
- our evaluation tools and frameworks are valid and reliable
- our frameworks are fair
- we aim to reduce inspection burdens and make our expectations and findings clear
- we target our time and resources where they can lead directly to improvement. (www.gov.uk/government/organisations/ofsted/about)

Inspection reports can be found on the Ofsted website by entering a school name or a postcode. Full inspection reports are accessible and clearly written with each school being graded on a four point scale – outstanding (1), good (2), requires improvement (3) or inadequate (4). Potential users of schools can construct a list for comparison, with a link being provided to the most recent inspection report and where the 1–4 outcome is highlighted. The rest of this chapter provides a critical exploration of the role of school inspection and of forms of metrics utilised in relation to education.

A CRITICAL STANCE

Ofsted has been subject to more substantial critical analysis from academics, professionals and trade unions than any other of the inspection bodies analysed in this book. The critical stances in relation to school inspection have been categorised here as follows and each will be examined in turn:

- the system is over-burdensome for schools
- the methods of measurement are unreliable or inaccurate
- the system is unfair to particular schools
- the system encourages gaming.

The system is over-burdensome for schools

First of all we explore the view that the system is over-burdensome for schools: our two teacher respondents shared this view as we shall see. The bureaucratic and burdensome nature of inspection is well documented by trade unions and professional bodies, and ironically by Ofsted itself in their 2020 Annual Report. In 2020 the National Education Union (NEU) stated that they believed, in relation to primary schools, that:

> Ofsted's new inspection framework has been designed with secondary school management structures in mind. It assumes a management structure of Heads of Department with responsibility for a subject area, with appropriate extra non-contact time which allows them to monitor the teaching of the subject and student progress, and appropriately rewarded with a Teaching and Learning Responsibility (TLR) payment ..... in most primary schools, teachers who are subject leads for a curriculum area do not have a timetable with additional non-contact time which would enable them to observe, assess and monitor the teaching of the curriculum in their subject area. (NEU 2019)

In addition to trade union and professional association critiques there are also political criticisms, for example, the British Labour Party stated in their 2019 election manifesto that, albeit with little contextual analysis:

> We will replace Ofsted and transfer responsibility for inspections to a new body, designed to drive school improvement. (Labour Manifesto 2019)

The origins of this proposal are to be found in a debate at the 2019 Labour Conference, during which the Finnish model was highly praised – a model we discuss later. In common with other respondents interviewed for this study, both of the teachers felt that the process was too haphazard:

> People get really nervous and twitchy in the build-up – not sure how that is good for children? ... You pray that the kids will behave and not play up, because kids will play up if they get a new audience. You too perform differently as you have an audience. (Respondent Five)

> It is a bit random to me: do they come on good day or bad day? Which inspector do you get? Will the kids behave that day? It then becomes randomness dressed up as science! (Respondent Six)

The internet, blogs and various books aimed at a wider audience provide critical accounts of inspections, elaborating on the quotes above. We utilise just two quotes to illustrate this theme, the first from a headteacher, the second from a classroom teacher:

> Ofsted creates an environment of fear, anxiety and worry for teachers. To prepare for an Ofsted visit, you may have to do a lot of tick-box exercises, regimented things that don't add value but help a school to look good. It inevitably adds to a teacher's workload. (Ferguson 2019)

> On the morning I found one Head of Year in tears and a brilliant Head of Department looking like he had not slept for 48 hours. Stress was kicking in: no one wanted their fiefdom to be the cause of the school dropping its outstanding tag. There was much less adrenaline and much more evident tension. Jokes were more gallows than guffaws and few people were anything other than frazzled.... The inspectors left, we collapsed and waited for the verdict .... I know how I felt over the days – stomach pains, little sleep, sweating, anxiety attacks. (*The Guardian* 2014)

This blog resonates with quotes from our two respondents:

> It is definitely a source of pressure, one or two staff will not cope and will go off sick, just before or on the first day. Sometimes we didn't see them for a number of weeks – three or four or five weeks. It is a distortion of normal school life, you will never get the true picture. (Respondent Five)

> I had sleepless nights before inspections – on top of working late into the evening before an inspection. The stress is enormous. (Respondent Six)

There are numerous sources that can be used to reinforce these points. One example is provided by this letter from Emeritus Professor Michael Bassey published in *The Guardian*:

> [Ofsted] has engendered fear in those inspected, and where it found fault, conveyed its criticisms to the public and parents in a way which could undermine confidence in the school and its head. The government should abolish Ofsted. (Bassey 2020)

The stress and ill-health brought about by the inspection process seems disproportionate: it is difficult to know why we would want to put a public servant through the fear outlined in this quote? In Ofsted's own survey 76%\ found the inspection process to be 'highly stressful for everyone' (Ofsted 2017). Our two teacher respondents back up the experience of stress outlined in their earlier quotes:

> Our school burnt down and we were working in mobile classrooms, in the middle of a building site, and it was a filthy winter: we had an inspection in the middle of this. They [Ofsted] said if you are open for business, you are open for inspection. In an existing building that had survived the fire, I put an exhibition on the staircase, we spent hours putting them up. To this day I am convinced that the inspector never looked at it, because some of the criticisms in his report were covered by the exhibition. The techniques and the gaps, as he saw them, were all there. (Respondent Five)

> I had numerous sleepless nights – worrying about the experience and any spin-offs from it. The School Leadership team put us under a lot of pressure: it was the worst part of the job – easily! (Respondent Six)

Returning to the experience of the school fire and the subsequent inspection, one of the respondents comments that:

> I was horrified, he [the inspector] had no idea of the trauma we had been through. For my subject in particular I lost lots of resources – I lost stuff I had been given for my 18th and 21st birthdays that had got messages in them from aunts and uncles. I was teaching with an empty bag, whilst feeling under pressure to be normal. It was a really cruel thing to do. (Respondent Five)

Even in these extreme circumstances the teacher becomes an object of inspection and subject to considerable stress. This respondent felt that of the inspectors, in general, 'weren't a "critical friend", they were just critical!' (Respondent Five). The same respondent stated that:

It was a pressure in the back of your mind all the time: it was horrendous, you could see people starting to look worried. You could feel the pressure in the corridors, working extra hours as they wanted it to look nice visually – as if it didn't anyway! You could hear the sound of staple guns in the corridors dawn to dusk! (Respondent Five)

Both the respondents felt that the pressure for positive inspection outcomes created divisions between the classroom teachers and the school leadership team. One respondent reflects as follows on the leadership team comments about her art displays:

I was happy to replace the vinyl covering on the exhibitions as I knew what was up there was good anyway, but it was like 'that has been up there a few weeks don't you think you should replace it?' Then you were asked 'are you sure you want that one up there?' The ones you put up were to give kids a boost and for children to know that I valued their work … You weren't allowed to even curate your own work. (Respondent Five)

You get the impression that the Head and the governors are so nervous about the outcome that they get quite authoritarian and start saying you must do that, you must do this by tomorrow and so on and so on. Most of the time the Head and the Deputies were really supportive and helpful: but this seemed to change when an inspection was due. They became tetchy and more dictatorial: It was 'do this', 'don't do that', all the time. (Respondent Six)

These points seem to resonate with a broader point made by Lipsky as follows:

The development of performance measures is critical to a bureaucratic accountability policy. Administrators make great effort to develop performance measures in order to control employees' behaviour. (1980: 165)

Ofsted inspection methodology and the leadership approach has changed over time – a full presentation of these numerous changes is beyond the scope of this chapter. One respondent reflects on these changes and their impact as follows:

The inspection system changed over the years, and I think it became even more rigorous. It was held over you like a big stick: it was always held over you, 'you must do this, you must do that'. It wasn't that you must do this because it is best for children, it was because it was what someone in authority wanted you to do. You couldn't always see the reason for what you were being asked to do. (Respondent Five)

In terms of one of the main themes of this book – how the audit culture strives to turn deeply human processes into objects – the two respondents comment as follows:

> These kids are being turned into machines, just to produce things for a display, rather than just because it was worthwhile. (Respondent Five)

> Everything is measured and assessed– I went into teaching to encourage and stimulate and you just end up getting given a grading! (Respondent Six)

These inspection processes seem inhumane and over-demanding but, in 2020, following the appointment of Amanda Spielman as Chief Inspector in 2017, there seems to have been a considerable change of tone: she called for a kinder, gentler Ofsted (Wilby 2018). So much so that, for example, the impact of inspections on teachers' wellbeing and stress is highlighted in Ofsted's annual report:

> The report … says: 'Teachers … reported that Ofsted inspections can affect well-being and stress levels, especially when senior leaders expect more administrative work in preparation or if they focus too much on data and exam results.' (Gibbons and Roberts 2020)

The methods of measurement are unreliable or inaccurate

The second area of critical analysis proposes that the methods of measurement are unreliable or inaccurate. Inconsistency of processes and outcomes is mentioned by many of our respondents. One of the teachers reflects as follows on a positive experience, but followed by a negative one:

> During an earlier inspection, you had to supply a lot of paperwork in advance. I wanted to convert a building into a 3D studio, I got a letter from an inspector introducing himself with a list of funding organisations with examples of what other schools had done and I thought that is someone who actually knows what art teaching is all about. In a more recent inspection we were all on alert, I checked all the lesson plans, not one inspector came anywhere near us: I don't know if they took notice of what was on the walls, that was the hardest one, and hurt the most. (Respondent Five)

Inconsistency of approaches by inspectors is also noted by a trade union leader, Mary Bousted of the National Education Union:

> We have inspectors with no subject expertise or experience making judgment on the intent, implementation and impact of the curriculum, which is now the lens through which the quality of education judgments are to be made. (Lightfoot 2020)

Sharing this point, one of the respondents recalls someone who was:

> A really friendly inspector, who used to teach the same subject as me. You could tell he understood the issues and asked the right questions. (Respondent Six)

The outcomes of the inspection reports seemed to be inconsistent and were perceived not to be fair:

> With some reports I thought, yes I agree we could improve there, but I have also found myself saying 'that is totally unfair'! (Respondent Six)

The EDSK publication *Requires Improvement* argues a similar point:

> As far back as 1996, Ofsted's research had shown that pairs of inspectors awarded different grades after observing the same lesson in 33%\ of cases. (EDSK 2019)

There are many critiques of the unreliability of audit methodology in education – here we focus in some detail on one highly regarded analysis by an esteemed team of social statisticians – Leckie and Goldstein – of a measure known as Progress 8. We outline this study at some length in acknowledgement of the significance of the study: we also use a number of direct quotes from their work as the argument draws on statistical analysis and is both complex and detailed. Leckie and Goldstein commence their study with an opening observation consistent with the main theme of this book:

> In the UK, US and elsewhere, education systems increasingly hold schools to account using school performance measures derived from pupil scores in high-stakes standardised tests and examinations. (Leckie and Goldstein 2019: 4)

They point out that England has been a leading force in the movement towards school-based accountability through the use of metrics:

> Successive governments over the last twenty-five years have introduced new and supposedly improved school performance measures that purport to measure what is happening in schools … These measures are also used to promote parental choice via their high-profile publication in 'school league tables' … They are also used by schools for self-evaluation, improvement, tracking, and target setting purposes, with schools increasingly buying in data analysis support from commercial organisations to assist them in these endeavours … The measures also inform national debates around regional inequalities, the performance of different school types, and performance gaps across socio-economic, ethnic, and other pupil groups. (Leckie and Goldstein 2019: 4)

Leckie and Goldstein explore the operation of a measure known as Progress 8, which is a 'value-added' approach, introduced as a measure of progress made by pupils between the end of primary schooling Key Stage 2 tests and the GCSE examinations. The score for each pupil is calculated as follows:

> Each pupil's score is calculated as their Attainment 8 score minus the average Attainment 8 score of all pupils nationally with the same KS2 prior attainment (KS2 scores are categorised into 34 groups for this purpose). A school's Progress 8 score is simply the average of their pupils' scores and is presented with a 95%\ confidence interval to communicate its statistical uncertainty. (Leckie and Goldstein 2019)

Given this form of analysis they argue that schools with more 'educationally advantaged' pupils in England would be expected to demonstrate higher average pupil Progress 8 scores compared to schools with an intake of less educationally advantaged intakes. The authors undertake sophisticated statistical analysis outlined as follows:

> we modified Progress 8, which only adjusts for pupil prior attainment, to produce an 'Adjusted Progress 8' measure that additionally accounts for seven further pupil characteristics: age, gender, ethnicity, language, Special Educational Needs, Free School Meals, and deprivation. We then compared Progress 8 and Adjusted Progress 8 in terms of schools' scores, ranks and classifications, and in terms of pupil average scores across a range of school characteristics. (Leckie and Goldstein 2019: 20)

They draw the following from the data:

> Our results for Progress 8 show that adjusting for pupil background qualitatively changes many of the interpretations and conclusions one draws as to how schools in England are performing. For example, over a third of schools judged 'underperforming' according to the Progress 8 floor standard would no longer be judged underperforming according to Adjusted Progress 8. More generally, a fifth of schools would see their national league table positions change by over 500 places ... Pupil FSM [free school meal eligibility] and ethnicity prove the most important characteristics to consider. For example, the high average pupil progress seen in London more than halves when we adjust for pupil background and this is principally due to the high proportions of high progress ethnic groups taught in London. In contrast, the low average pupil progress seen in the North East increases substantially after adjustment due to the disproportionately high proportions of poor pupils taught in this region. Other dramatic changes are seen for Grammar schools and faith schools whose high average pupil progress reduces substantially once the educationally advantaged nature of their pupils is taken into account. In contrast, the low average pupil progress seen in sponsored

academies increases once the disadvantaged nature of their pupils is recognised. (Leckie and Goldstein 2019: 21)

The failure of data driven assessment of schooling is summarised by the authors as follows, demonstrating an aspect of the unfairness of the system:

> In terms of Progress 8, the types of automated data-driven decision-making that the Government currently aspires to, whereby schools falling below a single floor standard are declared underperforming, cannot be supported by the data. (Leckie and Goldstein 2019: 23–24)

Elsewhere, the same authors conclude that the overall disadvantages driving school improvement through these metric-based approaches are as follows:

- Huge financial cost to implement
- Teaching time is taken up with the administrative burden of the tests
- The range of knowledge and skills that tests assess is very narrow
- Stress caused by over-testing turns children off education. (Leckie and Goldstein 2010)

In addition to these points it is worthwhile noting the position of secondary special schools, those serving pupils with special educational needs, produced by the league tables, which seems to enhance the stigma associated with such education. The lowest rated 400 of the 6,477 secondary schools are dominated by these special schools. There are 1,484 special schools in England in total and only one is rated above average: remarkably 1,483 special schools are rated below average or well below average. Paradoxically many of these schools have positive Ofsted reports. It seems then that league tables simply reflect existing status and differences and reproduce existing inequalities. This trend is also noteworthy in the league tables produced by commercial organisations such as the *Sunday Times*. They produce a league table of the *Top 424 Independent Secondary Schools*: the top 19 are all in the south of England, until one reaches Withington Girls' School at joint twentieth. Again existing inequalities are simply reflected in, and then reinforced by, the use of league tables. Nuala Burgess, a campaigner on these issues, argues powerfully as follows:

> League tables are a con. They rank schools on a very limited set of criteria that guarantee grammar schools come out on top ... It is time to put an end to the unfair practice of judging schools on grossly simplified data. There are lies, damned lies and league tables. If schools are to be ranked we need to produce a more holistic measure of what makes a good school. (Burgess 2021)

It can be argued that simply by doing away with the highly reductive grade and producing more nuanced narrative reports many of the issues associated with stress and inconsistency would be addressed – producing a more humane and analytical system producing learning rather than simplistic judgements.

The system is unfair to particular schools

The third argument often made by critics of metrics and the current school inspection system is that the system is unfair to particular schools. For example, Geoff Barton, leader of the Association of School and College Leaders (ASCL), argued that: 'Performance tables currently penalise schools which have more pupils in challenging circumstances. This is wrong' (Coughlan 2020).

This point is backed up by the experience of Akroydon primary academy in Halifax: despite demonstrable successes the school was graded as requires improvement by Ofsted. The headteacher argues in reference to a new Ofsted approach that:

> This is framework written over a middle class dinner table. Ofsted seems to think that if you can talk coherently about your curriculum then the results will look after themselves, but that is not going to happen at a school like ours, in areas of high deprivation. (Lightfoot 2020)

It has also been strongly argued that the inspection system struggles to analyse difference and innovation within the system, for example the free school movement and Steiner schools. In this context I explore the closure of a Steiner school in England following a highly critical Ofsted report. This led to a campaign to save the school, which is analysed by Richard House (2020) in his book entitled, *Pushing Back to Ofsted: Safeguarding and the Legitimacy of Ofsted's Inspection Judgements – A Critical Case Study*. The book explores and challenges the inspection and subsequent closure of a Steiner Waldorf Wynstones School, which was located in Gloucestershire, England. The final report on the school was published in early 2020. The author provides a critical analysis of two main issues in his study: first, the role of inspection, as embodied by Ofsted, and second, the emphasis on safeguarding – the main rationale provided leading to the closure of Wynstones. Here, we focus on House's critique of the inspection process. *Pushing Back to Ofsted* raises many issues about the inspection process, the role of the state in relation to alternative forms of education and the place of alternative educational approaches. The author provides succinct, direct quotes from the Ofsted report and follows this by his analysis of what happened during the process when the school was closing. This is followed by House's discussion and analysis, a very helpful selected bibliography in relation to Ofsted, the parental survey findings and concluding remarks from a former Steiner advisor. Richard House himself was a campaigner against the closure and a member of the Wynstones Parents' Core Group, and provides a highly committed alternative to the Ofsted view. *Pushing Back to Ofsted* provides a stimulating read and raises many key questions about how education is planned, delivered and inspected. House provides two core arguments: that the safeguarding paradigm is damaging and over-dominant and, our primary concern here, that the Ofsted methodology utilises values and methods that are bound to clash with the creative and holistic approach adopted in Steiner schools. However, my reading of the Ofsted report varies from that of Richard House as he argues that safeguarding was primary in Ofsted's concerns: my reading is that there was more emphasis on educational and leadership issues. In relation to Ofsted, House raises many critical issues about how we can perceive 'standards' and what is actually meant by the term 'evidence'. His argument is cogent and largely convincing: the school closure has caused considerable damage as evidenced by the results of the parental survey, which is included in the book. However, Ofsted evidence is rooted in some disturbing allegations, for example in respect of bullying by pupils: this would, of course, be wholly unacceptable if proven to have existed within the school, and would justify Ofsted's inspection and the subsequent action that was taken. Whilst I disagree with the main thrust of House's book it does raise challenging questions about how alternative forms of education can be inspected.

The system encourages gaming

The fourth critique of the current audit and metric system is that it encourages gaming of the system: this refers to schools taking particular actions as they improve the metrics without necessarily improving the education of the children and young people. Jerry Muller (2018) demonstrates how the system in the USA following on from the well-intentioned No Child Left Behind legislation led to gaming of the system. In the English context Leckie and Goldstein argue that:

> there has been a large rise in pupil exclusions over the last two years which in part has been attributed to schools gaming the accountability system in these ways. (2010: 7)

Geoff Barton, the ASCL leader we have already quoted, argued that:

> In our system, it is simply a fact that a small number of rogue results can send your Progress 8 score into nosedive. It is a perverse incentive to do the wrong thing and ease out the pupils in the margins. These will inevitably be the young

people who need the greatest support – vulnerable children who are struggling to cope. And when the stakes are so high – when careers and reputations hang in the balance – the temptation to find a way of gaming performance tables is also that much greater. (Schools Week 2020)

Ironically even the chief architects of the metrics systems – the Department of Education and Ofsted themselves – are concerned about gaming the system. In reference to the metric of achieving five GCSEs with a C grade or above it has been argued that:

> Ministers are worried that schools game the system by focusing their efforts on pupils on the borderline between a C and a D, while giving less attention to pupils who are on course to obtain a C or better. They also fear that pupils who appear to have little chance of achieving a C grade are being abandoned. Some schools have been accused of entering their students in subjects deemed to be 'soft' in the hope that they would achieve more C grades. (*The Times* 2013)

Ingram and colleagues interviewed teachers about their perspective on school performance and gaming and conclude that:

> Decisions made by schools on examination entry practices were consistently justified as being what was best for their students, and many of these decisions also benefited the school in terms of its portrayal in performance tables. Yet many of these same practices are also described as playing the system or gaming by participants in schools which made different decisions. (Ingram, Elliott, Morin, Randhawa and Brown 2018: 558)

Gaming is certainly an issue – but again it is encouraged by the use of reductive gradings and league tables.

ALTERNATIVE METHODS

Our teacher respondents had reflected on their experiences of the inspection system and how it perhaps could be improved:

> The old system of Local Authority advisors worked well, they knew the school and you felt comfortable with them. You didn't always agree with them, but they had a better insight. The advisors were useful – it was a two-way thing. They would provide help and advice. You could spot your own weaknesses. (Respondent Five)

> I can take on expert advice and I would love to work in this way – without the fear of being judged and seen as a failure. (Respondent Six)

This point resonates with that made by Professor Bassey in his letter published in *The Guardian* (7.2.2020):

> Local authority inspectors/advisers, aware of local factors on school performance, are all that are required. The government should realise how professionally committed teachers are to the children they teach and how hard they work … Advisory inspection may help: punitive inspection doesn't.

One teacher respondent favoured a peer review approach, a well-established system in some sectors:

> I would like a system that involved more frontline teachers – we could even swap mini-inspections teams that would share our realities and experiences. (Respondent Six)

They also desired a more shared, collective approach but felt that the introduction of more competitive approaches had undermined this:

> We had monthly meetings across the Local Education Authority, where we shared ideas but that has all gone by-the-by due to academisation: you don't get that sharing across schools. The collegiate approach has gone. (Respondent Five)

This is a direct result of the introduction of league tables and competition in the system. Reflecting the opposite of the audit culture and the implicit lack of trust, one respondent stated what she wished for:

> I'm of the view: leave teachers to do what they do best – don't interfere. (Respondent Five)

This is a theme throughout this book where competition has displaced productive forms of co-operation. A more co-operative learning environment echoes the much heralded Finnish system, which involved the abolition of a national inspection body:

> In most European countries, school inspection is still an important instrument for educational evaluation, but in Finland it was now completely abolished … Accordingly, whereas in many countries the inspection system holds schools accountable for achievements and makes these judgements about criteria and standards, the educational legislation reform of 1998 and the Finnish model for evaluating educational outcomes that was first introduced in the mid-1990s obliged the organisers of education to assess educational outcomes mainly locally. This means that the organisers of education, in most cases municipalities,

were given the main responsibility for monitoring the effectiveness of education and securing that every child has equal opportunities in proceeding through basic education. (Vainikainen, Thuneberg, Marjanen, Hautamäki, Kupiainen and Hotulainen 2017: 246)

Sally Wheale (2019) outlines the Finnish system where there is no national inspection, no streaming and no league tables and which is highly regarded internationally. Significantly, she describes teachers as being 'highly trained, revered and trusted'.

There are, therefore, alternatives to a strong, centrally led inspection model – where there is a focus on learning and development.

CONCLUSION

Mike Power makes the following point which gives us a springboard for drawing some conclusions from the arguments made above:

> Trow argues that while the creation of adequate procedures for complaints are important, teaching ultimately depends on appointing competent teachers whose motivation is independent of attempts to audit them. The performance culture of rewards and penalties is a refusal to trust this motivational guarantee with the result that teaching will be oriented to the expectations of the customer rather than shifting and transforming those expectations. (1997: 103)

The impact of inspection seems more visceral for the world of schools than in some of the other sectors we have explored. There are frequent references to sleepless nights and time off sick in the grey literature in particular. But we have seen that there are actually existing alternatives that emphasise learning, development and reflection over the competitive values championed by the audit culture.

5

CHILDREN'S SOCIAL CARE: MEASURING THE IMMEASURABLE

As well as the high profile role in schools, explored in the previous chapter, Ofsted is also responsible for the inspection of children's social care (CSC from here on). There are just over 150 CSC departments in England, with slightly different arrangements in Wales, and more significant organisational differences in Scotland and Northern Ireland. CSC deliver services for vulnerable children and young people aged under 18 and work with them up to the age of 25 when they have been in local authority care. Services include providing early help, child protection, children's disability services, adoption, fostering and provision for children looked after by the local authority. They must appoint an accountable officer, usually designated as a Director of Children's Services (DCS) and a named lead from amongst the elected members. CSC have been subject to a number of inspection regimes since they have fallen within the remit of Ofsted. Whatever the details of the regime the inspections have been intensive and rigorous – subjecting CSC to high standards of accountability and measurement (Hood Nilsson and Habibi 2019). It is in this field that the majority of my experience falls and my observations of these inspection systems provided the primary motivation in writing this book. I have witnessed first-hand intensive preparation, apprehension approaching fear about forthcoming inspections, flurries of activity around inspections which paralyse the leadership team, deflated morale and chaos following negative judgements. A negative inspection outcome – as we will hear first from two respondents – leads to chaos, dismissal and resignations, periods of instability, intense media and political scrutiny and, quite often, a deterioration in the performance indicators which may have concerned Ofsted in the first place. This process will be explored in some detail – an experience which will be illustrated by the first-hand accounts of our two CSC respondents. In order to build our argument, the focus here is on negative experiences of inspections – but it should be noted that positive outcomes are more frequent and other respondents would have provided different narratives around the experience. I wanted to provide a voice for this dysfunctional element of the inspection process – I have found no other comparable academic accounts.

MEASURING THE IMMEASURABLE

There have been a number of methodologies adopted by Ofsted to inspect CSC. The transition from the SIF (Single Inspection Framework) to the most recent system at the time of writing, the ILACS (Inspection of Local Authority Children's Services), is described by Ofsted (2019: 3) as follows:

> Under the SIF, we delivered a standard four-week inspection to all Local Authorities (LAs). The ILACS framework is a more complex system of inspection. Our aim was to create a proportionate inspection process based on intelligence gathered throughout the year. The main differences between the SIF and ILACS frameworks are:
>
> - a move from a universal, four-week inspection to a more tailored inspection menu, which includes: – LA self-evaluations of social work practice – annual engagement meetings with LAs – focused visits (two days on-site) – monitoring visits of inadequate LAs (two days on-site) – joint targeted area inspections (JTAIs) – short (one week) and standard (two week) inspections
> - more frequent, individualised contact with LAs to regularly assess risks and improvements
> - less focus on processes and a greater focus on social work practice: in practical terms, this is a shift from a greater number of meetings that made up SIF inspections to the aim of inspectors spending 80% of their time talking to social workers and directly observing practice
> - inspection teams working together to collect, collate and evaluate evidence in all strands being inspected or reviewed: evidence collection and evaluation was much more individualised in SIF inspections
> - shorter, more concise inspection reports that aim to provide clear direction on areas for improvement rather than covering all evaluation criteria
> - LIs being more involved in evidence gathering in ILACS inspections: this is alongside leading the team, dealing with the necessary administration and being responsible for inspection quality (with support from quality assurance managers (QAMs)).

Reports are published in full with the graded outcomes on the Ofsted website.

CSC, their social workers and other care staff deliver complex services to children and young people who have been abused, neglected, abandoned or who experience some form of disability. It is hard work (I did it for eight years) and your best intentions may be met by verbal, and occasionally physical, abuse. Practitioners make complex and demanding decisions everyday – maybe without enough time to really think issues through, probably without sufficient resources and sometimes with a lack of background material. The primary legislation in the arena, the Children Act 1989, simultaneously demands that these staff keep families together where possible and separates children from their families where this is judged appropriate. I have argued elsewhere that this situation is best summed up by one word – 'complexity' (Frost 2021). As one of the respondents comments:

> They want it to be simple but the complexity of the work is not matched by the Ofsted lens. (Respondent Six)

Ferguson and his team reflect on the process of evidence gathering as follows:

> Inspectors placed a great deal of emphasis on how they sought to evaluate services by triangulating the evidence they had obtained from a variety of sources – including case files, interviews with social workers, audits, performance data, and so on. However, the vast majority of the evidence gathered did not include the direct experiences of service users, so evaluation was done at a distance from, and without consultation with, the very people the data that was being triangulated was about. Impact was sometimes interpreted as a measurable variable, usually meaning the focus was on an organisational outcome rather than the experience of the child. (Ferguson, Gibson and Plumbridge 2019: 47)

How then can this complexity be measured and judged? Inevitably the process involves simplification – Ofsted judgements at the time of writing are as follows: inadequate, requires improvement, good and outstanding. These one or two word judgements summarise the mix of difficult and demanding activity taking place in, for example, a city riven by poverty, inequality and other social divisions. One simplification is that children and young people are reduced to 'outcomes', passive objects who can be measured: outcomes is the dominant concept in the field. Of course, those of us that are parents or aunts and uncles have never thought of children and young people as 'outcomes': it is something that children of the state become so they can be audited and measured, in the spirit of governmentality discussed in Chapter 1.

BRUISED, CONFUSED AND UNDERMINED: TWO NARRATIVES OF INSPECTION

I undertook two interviews with senior managers who had experienced negative inspection outcomes: their experiences are reported in some detail below and their accounts gel with my own experiences in a number of roles. The intention was to highlight the effect of the negative impacts: but it is worthy of repetition that there are also those who feel positive about their inspection process, but the intention here is to build a critical narrative and to give a voice to those voices that are rarely heard.

Both of the respondents started with significant experience of, and some positive views in relation to, inspections:

> I have always welcomed inspections, I have had some positive feedback from inspections. (Respondent Five)

> Inspections have been part of my professional life it feels like forever: they have certainly been around in the more senior part of my career forever ... Business often got organised around the requirements of an inspection – which isn't all bad, as it all drives you towards improved outcomes for children. You would examine complaints, examine care planning and look at outcomes which was positive, but a number of things were not positive. (Respondent Six)

They both found the experience of inspections stimulating, if sometimes mystifying:

> We had an [Her Majesty's Inspectors of Prisons and Ofsted] inspection with six sections – good in all of them and one requires improvement [RI] – I challenged the inspector, as it felt it was arbitrary and I couldn't for the life of me understand the RI. We had one in about 2011 of Youth Justice and we got one of the best in the country – outstanding in every section. It was immense for [the authority] and I still dine out on it now. But what irks me to this day [is] the grading [from] HMIP [which] was minimum improvement needed– how could you celebrate when we have got minimum improvement needed! It was irksome and a kick in the teeth for staff. (Respondent Five)

The other respondent noted that the impact of audit and inspection had grown over the years, thus illustrating a major theme of this book:

> Over the years the inspection regime gradually took on more and more of a determining factor in how one led the business ... Inspection grew from something that was quite little to something that was dominant. (Respondent Six)

The respondents, in common with senior professionals throughout the country, had a good sense of their own services and had engaged in significant preparation. They had little choice but look at themselves through the Ofsted lens and to 'self-assess':

> We would self-assess ourselves, on the back of the ex-Ofsted consultants' work, as between 'requires improvement' and 'good'. (Respondent Five)

> I did a lot of work to establish good demand management and performance data from which … the performance team and I predicted inadequate in a couple of areas due to a range of issues including high caseloads, staff turnover, etc. (Respondent Six)

These quotes illustrate one of Foucault's themes around governmentality – the subject becomes an active partner in the process of surveillance and measurement. Whilst this preparation is speculative, extensive and expensive, the atmosphere goes up by many notches when the expected phone call from Ofsted is received:

> In 2018 the phone rings, it was the Lead Inspector and we pressed the button. I felt we knew ourselves well – and all was OK, not perfect, but OK. (Respondent Five)

The demands of this emotional process on both the inspectors and the objects of those inspections are noted by Ferguson et al. as follows:

> Thus the emotional demands of inspections are great, not only on agencies but also on inspectors and the impact of this requires careful thought. Because the stakes are so high, and inspection is an intense, anxiety provoking experience, inspectors have to deal with both their own emotions and those of the local authority and have to help them manage them. (2019: 63)

The respondents views of the inspectors were mixed, with some regarded highly and others seen as behaving poorly:

> I was involved in [an inspection with an] inadequate [judgement] and one outstanding, I was substantially involved and we were delighted. There were loads of positive comments – but it was a tense relation with the inspectors. I had three 'one-to-ones' … and they were civil but one in particular I didn't warm to his style: he was like a police officer trying to catch you out. He would say 'I have heard that …', he was trying to lull you into a false sense of security … I thought that was poor behaviour. I thought it was cynical. (Respondent Five)

The Lead Inspector plays a key role and is central to the experience:

> The Lead Inspector I found very difficult. We had a JTAI less than a year before – where they had no concerns. We had the ex-inspector who spent a lot of time with us with no reflections of note. But then the Lead Inspector has grave concerns. That feels like your hands are tied behind your back, the LI was sneering, rude, and I felt he enjoyed the critical aspect and enjoyed making us uncomfortable. His manner and approach was fundamentally unhelpful. The second in command never said a word, the Lead Inspector was absolutely domineering. (Respondent Five)

> The outcomes of the inspection would often depend on the approach of Lead Inspector. If you had a good, experienced and well-informed inspector, then they were more likely to successfully negotiate the complexities of the stuff that happens in children's social care. You could say this child has had seven or eight placements, then they ran away and this placement is nearer home, so it isn't ideal, but it is working and they would say fine … Some of it felt like it was your luck on the day, depending on who the team and the Lead Inspector was. (Respondent Six)

Behind the mask of objectivity and scientific measurement there seems to be an element of chance and subjectivity. Ferguson et al. note this issue following their ethnographic research with inspectors:

> Generally speaking, we found consistency in the methods used to implement ILACS, although there was significant variation in approach in how these methods were applied to gathering data/evidence and in the interpretation of evidence. (Ferguson et al. 2019: 45)

One respondent had reflected on the variable nature of the experience and concluded that there was a lack of scientific method:

> I have felt supported when the inspection team took a positive and more collaborative approach and it was positive, but some were a hellish experience, it felt like they had come in to find you inadequate. They come in with a reductionist, glass half empty approach, which felt unfair to my staff and I. There was also a sense that there wasn't much scientific methodology behind their approach: you can ask 'can you evidence how you came to that conclusion?' There was nothing to suggest a robust methodical approach, that you could safely apply and make robust judgements comparing different authorities. (Respondent Six)

Ferguson and colleagues offer a related finding:

> Our observations found that relying so heavily on case files meant that the focus of inspectors was heavily on how well social workers and managers represent what they do in writing and on the administration and organisation of social work practice. (Ferguson et al. 2019: 50)

Both respondents felt that the negative judgements they received had a significant impact on both staff and services:

> I regret deeply what happened to the council as a result of inspection and it moved the authority backwards, as well as having a substantial personal impact on myself. I do understand that the purpose of inspection is to hold a mirror to yourself, but the way this was done drove the authority backwards. (Respondent Five)

> In the end the politicians and the Chief Executive desperately wanted to be outstanding, or at the very least good, but would not put in the resources, or prioritise, or even listen to the complexity of what the whole Local Authority would have to do collectively across the council and the safeguarding partnership, it was all put on to you as Director of Children's Services (DCS). It was your job to make it happen. It is of course the DCS's job as statutory officer to lead service improvement, however, the efforts of a DCS alone in a context that does not support the vision for children and the commitment necessary to achieve these means that the DCS is working with one hand behind their backs … A friend of mine says that Children's Social Care is like the canary in the mine, if Children's Services are in difficulty that generally means the council is in difficulty. (Respondent Six)

The negative impact was therefore on service delivery but was also deeply personal: damaging the confidence of what I would regard as high quality, very committed and long-standing professionals who had made the choice to work with vulnerable children. A system based on trust would recognise that such people would perform to the best of their ability. They would welcome guidance, new research findings and a helpful steer – but why should they be subject to brutal audit regimes which could find them and their best efforts 'inadequate'?

The respondents had a sound knowledge of their own services based in audits, experience and professional judgements. One of the respondents had a positive inspection, shortly before a later devastating one:

> With the JTAI [Joint Targeted Area Inspection] into domestic violence I was central to it: I did a lot of work, was part of the self-assessment and sent off evidence

in advance. Then a massive team of about 13 inspectors arrived – from Ofsted, CQC, HMIC, HMIP and the inspection was very forensic. Three or four inspectors were all over our 'front door' for four days – looking at domestic violence and following the journey of the child. It was absolutely forensic and they went here, there and everywhere. We got phenomenal feedback from the inspectors in relation to our 'front door' processes and, of course domestic violence was far and away the biggest referral issue. Ofsted feedback was that we were good, really, really strong. They said our MASH [Multi-Agency Safeguarding Hub] was very strong ... My director at the time took the Lead Inspector into a room and said about the JTAI if it was an ILACS [Inspection of Local Authority Services] we would have got 'good' towards 'outstanding' – we were buzzing. (Respondent Five)

Yet 18 months later some of these very same services were judged negatively by Ofsted.

It is argued here that one unintended consequence of a poor inspection outcomes goes like this:

- Authority A has a negative inspection, say, relating to high staff turnover or large caseloads.
- Authority A then offers a good recruitment package: perhaps including golden handshakes, advanced career progressions and so on.
- Social workers leave neighbouring Authority B to work for Authority A as a result of the enhanced employment packages.
- Authority B then experiences high staff turnover and large caseloads – a negative inspection may then follow for this authority.

The inspection system then generates unintended consequences. This scenario is not imagined, as one respondent outlined:

One issue we had was because (a neighbouring local authority) went inadequate they went into turmoil, into meltdown, and started throwing money at recruiting social workers. They started paying extra to agency staff and they gave a golden hello and a retention allowance, you could leave us and get a £7k pay rise and £2k in their pocket, and several of our social workers converted to agency work and moved. We lost 30 social workers to a neighbouring authority in total. (Respondent Five)

Another challenge for CSC is the variety of inspection types and the changing inspection regimes – making transfer of learning very difficult. Despite this, preparation is meticulous and expansive, as one respondent outlines:

When the new ILACS was announced I went to conferences and seminars put on by Ofsted. We realised we had work to do – but our systems remained the same as the recent JTAI. No wheel had fallen off … we wanted to make sure we got a good ILACS. Another local authority recommended an ex-Ofsted inspector to undertake a mock inspection under the ILACS framework … he did about 20 days of work in total – three or four days in 'front door', etc. He charged around £750 per day – there is a lot of money to be made on the back of being an ex-Ofsted inspector! He found some slight weaknesses but although he spent several days in our 'front door' he identified no substantive issues about our operation, no issues about strategy meetings, no issues about consent: just some minor recommendations. (Respondent Five)

Once the inspection begins the respondents start a process of reading inspector behaviour and assessing feedback. One respondent outlines this and feels that the process is subjective:

By day two I knew it was starting to go wrong. The Lead Inspector went into the 'front door' which I thought was a clear strength – but the Lead Inspector had a different narrative about the Early Help and 'front door' set up – he didn't like it. It was the same set up as an outstanding rated local authority but he didn't like it. He felt that we were doing too many assessments and that we were getting assumed consent rather than actual consent. He didn't like us having so many police officers – he refused to understand that our CSE [child sexual exploitation] team was located within the 'front door' which was why there were so many police officers on the floor. He saw our 'front door' as 'police led' and that we were too quick to go into police records and health records. He had a 'bee in his bonnet' about this and he crucified us. (Respondent Five)

The reader will be able to sense the frustration of the respondent: an earlier inspection had been positive, meticulous preparation had taken place, self-assessment had taken place, but still a negative downward spiral occurs. One of my respondents from the police, who had experience of working with CSC colleagues on inspections, refers to periods of 'paralysis' during Ofsted inspections. A single case found by inspectors can be used to evidence a negative finding:

[the inspector] brought up a case … where the child was on an Early Help plan with Family Support workers going in twice a week … that child was being seen on a regular basis. He deliberately mis-reported it that the child was not being seen despite the fact that we evidenced that he was being seen … yet he still used this as an example to the Chief Executive and to elected members … it looked bad, but not when you knew the details. He was sneering, unhelpful and looking to find fault. (Respondent Five)

The non-social work reader should be aware that social work is an inexact professional activity: five different highly able professionals may come up with five
different, but highly appropriate plans, for the same situation. The inspector of
the case outlined above is assuming a perfect model which all should adhere
to: after 40 years of social work practice, teaching and research I am unaware of
such a fool-proof model. A similar example happened in relation to the system
for children and young people in state care (Looked After Children):

> They looked at Looked After Children. I knew what an outstanding team we
> had. In my view it was good, I would put us above [a well-regarded local author-
> ity], in all sincerity. Staff went the extra mile, they were amazing with a brilliant
> manager. We were 98% on undertaking PEPs [Personal Education Plans], etc.,
> I honestly thought it was good. Some inspectors went in and it seemed to be
> going well. The tone just changed: I am convinced the Lead Inspector sets the
> tone and the others fall in behind him. (Respondent Five)

As the judgements are subjective it follows that different inspectors may have
differing views. Respondent Five outlines how one inspector seemed to be
highly impressed but apparently was over-ruled by the Lead Inspector:

> We had a complex case, the inspector was in tears – crying, because the work
> was outstanding that the Social Worker and the Team Around the Child had
> done. The inspector was so moved by the work of the social worker that she
> actually hugged her. Yet, later that day, the Lead Inspector, when asked if he
> had seen anything good in the Looked After Children [LAC] team, stated that
> it was some of the most shocking work he had ever seen! He only conceded
> that he had seen 'one or two bits of good work': his attitude was shocking.
> We got 'requires improvement' for LAC and Child Protection – I am very expe-
> rienced and stand by our self-assessment that we should certainly have been
> rated 'good' for LAC and probably been rated 'good' for our work with children
> in need of help and protection. (Respondent Five)

The hegemony of inspection then has tremendous power: subjective opinions
become objective judgements; the perspective of one professional undermines
that of another, perhaps more competent, professional; careers and morale are
destroyed on the basis of a single case, as we have seen in the quote above.
The service that Respondent Five was responsible for was devastated by the
outcome of the inspection:

> It was shocking for our staff, but it felt like it was just a game to him. The Looked
> After Children team were buzzing from their day-to-day experience of being
> inspected but this was not reflected in the written report and the Lead Inspector

sought to make mincemeat of the 'front door' and our procedures. It was brutal: we were left reeling and, of course, had to keep this confidential while waiting for the draft report to come. (Respondent Five)

Similar experiences are reported by the other respondent:

There was an 'inadequate' judgement. My management team were distraught and I was in touch with them most days, it was devasting for everyone. It was painful – at least I would have been able to contextualise the situation … The authority was found overall inadequate, it was devastating for everyone, it was very painful for me even though I had left. I am pretty confident that I could have held it or the outcome would not have been so negative, if I was there. (Respondent Six)

One respondent notes a disjunction between the content and tone of the report and the summarising of the dedicated work of professionals as, quite simply, 'inadequate':

[it was the] nicest inadequate report I have ever read, it didn't feel too bad – so the overall 'inadequate' judgement felt like it was part of a power trip and it was a big blow to everyone. (Respondent Five)

The competence of the inspection team was brought into question by the occurrence of:

massive, glaring factual errors which we had pointed out at the time and we again challenged and they accepted and made some changes. (Respondent Five)

The detail of the report was also highly questionable:

They said that our way of gaining consent was illegal – but we hadn't changed one thing from the JTAI and the ex-Ofsted inspector who undertook our mock inspection did not pick this up. Our 'front door' processes were actually just like those of [a well-regarded authority]. (Respondent Five)

The aftermath of the inspection process is profound and highly questionable. The inspection process does not stop when the final report is published:

The report gets published and the Director of Children's Services said, 'I have had enough', and he left: it broke him. He had been a DCS for a long period of time with many good and outstanding inspection reports behind him. It absolutely broke him – he fell on his sword. (Respondent Five)

The experienced senior managers do what they can to manage the process and the fall-out for more junior staff:

> We got all the staff together and brought out the positives. The improvements to the 'front door' that we needed to make to comply with Ofsted recommendations were relatively straightforward. (Respondent Five)

> I was absolutely dumbstruck by what I read (in the Commissioner's report). A colleague said I was collateral damage ... It was damning of me and my watch – that does not mean I do not take responsibility for what happened on my watch – I absolutely do. It was just not possible for me and my team to achieve what we wanted in that context and in hindsight I should have recognised that earlier. I said to the Commissioner that I had been given a draft, he took virtually nothing on board, even factual inaccuracies. I felt and feel hugely scapegoated. (Respondent Six)

But now we come to the crunch: the aftermath involves resignations, temporary staff, low morale, spiralling costs and the 'outcomes' criticised by Ofsted become even worse. There are many examples from our respondents:

> Then an Interim DCS was appointed and this is where things absolutely spiral. If the old DCS had actually stayed we could have easily turned it around and made it work. The interim DCS was ... on over £1,000 per day. I got some informal feedback from another authority where she was an interim DCS and they warned me that 'she will come in, declare things to be worse than first thought, clear staff out, bring in a team of interims, cause chaos and quickly leave' – and that is exactly what she did over a period of just three months. She came in ... and developed a narrative of 'this is the worst I have ever seen ... but I know the person for the job'. It was interim appointment after interim appointment ... performance people came in where it was absolutely unclear what their remit, authority or accountability was. Many were on £800 or so a day ... then they go and leave a mess behind. (Respondent Five)

Here the picture is familiar to people experienced in CSC. A critical report is followed by turmoil in senior appointments, highly paid interims with a low-commitment to a geographic area, an increase in expenditure and declining quality of care for children, young people and their families. This is a supreme irony as a result of the organisation designed to guarantee and maintain quality.

Both the respondents also highlighted the competitive environment, the back-biting and the acidic atmosphere that arose from those taking over so-called failing services. Managers are keen to perform to the Ofsted drama and to buy in to the dominant audit culture.

We went to a benchmarking meeting ... and we presented for peer review and I presented our data which in all honesty wasn't any better or any worse than most other local authorities in the region – but the interim DCS stated that the data from our LA was the worst she had ever seen, was disparaging of the previous DCS and said that the political support was the worst she had ever seen and I was squirming ... the audience was peer Directors of Children's Services and Assistant Directors and what she said was inaccurate. (Respondent Five)

This is a downside of the performance regimes that I have witnessed across a range of organisations: the narrative is that I am the saviour of this organisation and that I can turn it around because the previous regime was truly awful. Both the respondents had experience of this phenomena:

I quickly realised that this was her style and she had a huge vested interest in lowering the baseline – so she can say look what I have done – or any failure to deliver could be explained by saying 'things are even worse than Ofsted discovered'. (Respondent Five)

The dynamic in CSC now feels increasingly really competitive, where you are consistently criticised, the next DCS says it is rubbish here and the last DCS was rubbish too. (Respondent Six)

Respondents felt that the service declined rapidly following negative inspections:

It was a method of manipulation, but she was only there three to four months and did huge damage. She suggested a huge programme of change with interims brought in to deliver these – I thought some of the change programmes she instigated were crazy given she only intended to be there for three months. (Respondent Five)

There are three key themes that emerge from the wreckage of these damaging inspections: churn and turnover of staff; increased expenditure; and a decline in service delivery.

Let us examine each in turn commencing with staff change and turnover:

There were around 30 interim managers ... a stack of auditors, change managers, performance people ... the staff were reeling, they didn't know which direction they were going ... this was at a time that our staff needed direction and stability ...There has been a negative impact and it is no better off and is still in turmoil. Interims, it's human nature, they work hard but they aren't there for the longevity, so do not look for long-term organisational benefit. (Respondent Five)

Both respondents had argued before the inspections for increased expenditure and been refused or had experienced cut-backs. Ironically a negative inspection leads to increased expenditure:

> The service had lost its confidence … everything became risk averse … the council put back in £20m plus so in the end libraries and museums have closed … Afterwards in terms of resources it went crazy … we did appoint a fourth head of service for the 'front door', and agency workers on £500 or £600 per day. Then the DCS went and brought in an interim DCS at over £1,000 per day and she, in turn, brought in a whole team of interims with her. Contrast agency spent 2018–19 you would find an increase of more than £1m – the increase wasn't about frontline workers, it was about audit and management, I can see the logic but the social workers and the team leaders were reeling, the frontline staff didn't know if they were coming or going and were crying out for stability and direction. There was a stack of auditors coming in. The agency staff … their longevity was not great and people were just reeling. (Respondent Five)

Declining service delivery followed from negative inspection findings, illustrated as follows:

> Looked After Children numbers whacked up massively – Child Protection and Referrals all went up … The service is still reeling, and has still not bedded down with the coming and going of interims … they have been scared out of innovation into compliance, compliance, compliance. It caused chaos and ructions … I agree that you need to hold a mirror up – peer reviews are very helpful and very challenging. I have undertaken peer reviews … the system is very good, it is really, really positive, people make robust recommendations without the fear of you losing your job. I have been involved in focused visits, they are really powerful tools, you are held in account to the highest standard, you get a robust action plan but it doesn't send you into chaos. If we have a focused inspection on the 'front door' and he said I don't like this, or consent or early help and the police, it wouldn't have been a deal breaker. We would have said thank you and taken the action according to the action plan … it wouldn't have cost millions. (Respondent Five)

The impact is also very significant for the leaders who are implicated by Ofsted in so-called poor performance:

> My point here is the loss of experience and expertise to the child protection system – it cannot be right that colleagues and I having done 30 plus years of effective work in child care are 'cast out' … So children in effect are becoming less safe as experienced senior leaders either step back or find it hard to get senior jobs again – in which other profession does this happen – very few … Where

is the learning from experience, where is the valuing of skill and experience – what are we doing? It seems to me we are turning a blind eye. The pipeline to replace us is diminishing as social workers have on average an eight year professional life and diminishing … so are we unconsciously creating a situation where the people who occupy more senior roles are less equipped to do so as they are being promoted early and without what was once seen as longevity of experience … if this is the case then how safe are our children going forward? (Respondent Six)

Instead of Directors of Children's Services knowing it is a really hard role and knowing that on a bad day you are so close to the edge, so why not stand by somebody or at least not rubbish them and from there highlight how much better they will be in this role. What is that dynamic and what is fuelling it? The improvement teams that come in post-inspections, some are highly variable – some fine and some incompetent and not very skilled, with a narrative [where] they say you are all [rubbish] here. They look down and quash creativity and talent: what is happening in the profession … it is like a contagion. Everyone in the service is seen as rubbish – as a result my whole management team left, with tons of interims coming in, all on big daily fees! (Respondent Six)

The impact of the inspections was not only organisational but also deeply personal:

I felt bruised and that my reputation was trashed … I was not sleeping properly. (Respondent Five)

I had a great team, phenomenal in hindsight, and we were holding together the impossible: working early morning to late night in a crazy attempt to hold it together with too few social workers and support staff, due to austerity and the resultant savings context. I was waiting for my husband to fall asleep so I could do the days emails so I could support the staff to keep children safe. There was a big savings context, everything had been cut back. (Respondent Six)

I asked for £5m before the inspection and something like [many millions of pounds] had to go in in the end. Children are lost in all of this: it is the antithesis of our values as social workers. For me it was traumatic, it was dreadful. One morning I had the thought I could throw myself in front of a train. The shame that should belong to the institution and it is placed on you as an individual. You end up scapegoating yourself. If I didn't have a loving family and friends I could have stepped in front of a train. It is nothing more than an illusion, with a scapegoating process. The scapegoating is a big dent in your confidence. (Respondent Six)

These reflections are moving and profound. A related point was made by Ferguson and his team in research commissioned by Ofsted, which suggested that they should find:

ways of minimising the painful effects of judgements on local authorities, preventing feelings of blame and humiliation and helping them to deal with the consequences are clearly vital. (Ferguson et al. 2019: 64)

The two respondents summarised the experience as follows:

There is a role of scrutiny and inspection but the way it is done is self-defeating and damaging. It wasn't a car crash and they [Ofsted] made it a car crash. (Respondent Five)

This is my hypothesis – the system is built on, or emerged insidiously from, Ofsted's years of evaluation: we as Local Authorities and increasingly in the social work profession, at least at a senior level, then swallow them, the Ofsted judgements, whole without digesting them, questioning them or unpicking the meaning – you are either top of the ladder or at the bottom of the Ofsted judgement ladder. If you are at the top you are chosen for projects and extra resource. If you are 'requires improvement' or 'inadequate' you have all the sins on your back and there is a belief that there can't be anything good here in the authority. It has become a simple narrative – one where not only are some in my profession not questioning the narrative but are themselves making capital through reinforcing that narrative with their behaviour. The alternative is taking a systemic perspective, removing and/or reducing the personalisation, acknowledging that the outgoing DCS must take accountability and that going forward in the role they will work to support the context to make the necessary changes – a graceful and humble approach – that is what we are lacking. (Respondent Six)

CONCLUSION

What has been outlined here is a sad story of highly motivated and skilled professionals being undermined by an inefficient, expensive and brutal system of inspection. It does not pretend to be representative but it is a genuine narrative and a rarely explored issue. The critique can be summarised as follows:

- Ofsted are trying to audit and measure very complex and demanding professional work.
- This complexity has been reduced to a series of one or two word judgements.
- The nature of inspections and inspectors themselves is variable and this has an impact on inspection outcomes.
- There is a serious unintended consequence that authorities labelled 'inadequate' devise attractive packages that lead to staff moving from one authority to another, leaving other authorities short-staffed.
- There is a serious personal impact on highly skilled professionals who have spent their lives working with vulnerable children and young people.

- As senior managers are asked to 'perform' to Ofsted criteria they over invest in this and become critical of predecessors.
- The service itself seems to deteriorate – due to leadership changes, the use of interims, declining staff morale, fear of risk-taking and an over-emphasis on compliance.

The impact of this process on Children's Social Care seems to be high profile and profound. There is an alternative to this damaging system, which will be discussed in the final chapter of this book. As Hood and colleagues comment:

> It is in helping local authorities to carry out this function [of developing learning] rather than in punishing and rewarding their performance, that inspectors may find a more comprehensive role. (2016: 52)

CRIME AND POLICING: HOLDING THE POLICE ACCOUNTABLE

Of the five case studies that make up the bulk of this book the issue of public accountability is perhaps at its sharpest in the field of policing. The police are empowered to use force against citizens and have the power to detain in custody: therefore accountability is both a vital and often high profile issue (Rowe 2020). Lack or absence of police accountability is a hallmark of a totalitarian society. The issue of police accountability became internationally controversial during the Black Lives Matter protests of 2020. Black Lives Matter was founded in 2013, following the death of Trayvon Martin, a black American citizen. Black Lives Matter protests spread to many parts of the globe following the murder of George Floyd on 25 May 2020 in Minnesota, USA. The demands of Black Lives Matters included the de-funding of the police and the transfer of resources to more accountable, local community-based organisations (see blacklivesmatter. com): this makes the issues explored here particularly important and controversial. Police accountability is complex and varies internationally but there can be little doubt that, as Muller argues, in the USA context:

> policing has been transformed in recent decades by the use of metrics … here too the stakes are high: the fate of cities rests in no small part on the public's perception of its safety, and mayors often stake their re-election on their ability to bring down the crime rate. (2018: 125)

Systems of accountability and, in particular, the use of inspections and metrics will be examined here. As in the four other case studies in this book, interviews have taken place with two senior, experienced professionals in order to illustrate and inform some of the key themes.

The police exist inside a very complex web of accountability in England which involves the Home Office, the regional elected Police and Crime Commissioners (PCCs from here on), Her Majesty's Inspectorate of Constabulary and Fire and Rescue Services (HMICFRS from here on) and the Independent Office for Police Conduct (IOPC from here on). Accountability is particularly important as police officers exercise considerable power as, to utilise Lipsky's phrase, street-level bureaucrats:

> A central reason why police accountability is both challenging and necessary is that individual police officers have considerable scope to exercise discretion as they go about their duties. (Rowe 2020: 13)

The issue is complicated as the police, whilst being accountable, also need to be operationally independent from politicians, as stated in the Policing Protocol Order (2011) Article 30:

> The operational independence of the police is a fundamental principle of British policing. It is expected by the Home Secretary that the professional discretion of the police service and oath of office give surety to the public that this shall not be compromised.

We will explore this web of accountability utilising the perspectives of our two police experienced respondents. One of the respondents describes the system as being:

> complex with the Chief Constable, and then the PCC, who holds the Chief Constable to account, so it is not as direct in the police as in Children's Social Care … in the police it is more like accumulation and one poor result would not do for a Chief Constable, particularly a new one, or an Assistant Chief Constable, but it would accumulate: if I am honest I haven't seen examples of Chief Constables walking the plank, but usually they can go at the whim of the PCC. (Respondent Nine)

Since this interview was undertaken there has indeed been an example of a Chief Constable resigning, in December, 2020, following an inspection of the crime recording system in Greater Manchester (Britton 2020).

INSPECTION SYSTEMS

As in our four other case studies, inspection plays a crucial role – although perhaps these inspections have a lower profile than those of schools and children's social care, for example. The inspection task is carried out by the HMICFRS, which took over from Her Majesty's Inspector of the Constabulary (HMIC) following the Police and Crime Act 2017. HMICFRS (2018) explain their role as follows:

Our purpose

- To promote improvements in policing and fire & rescue services to make everyone safer.

Our values

- **Respect** – we respect and value all those we work with, and the contribution that they make.
- **Honesty** – we are truthful at all times.
- **Independence** – we are objective in all we do, without bias towards or against anyone: we are independent of the police service, fire & rescue authorities and government, and act only in the public interest.
- **Integrity** – we act ethically and openly in all we do.
- **Fairness** – we treat everyone – both within and outside HMICFRS – fairly.

Our objectives

- Demonstrate our values in everything we do.
- Conduct informed, independent and evidence-based inspections.
- Provide value for money.
- Work with others to promote improvements in policing and fire & rescue services.
- Report our inspection findings/analysis in a clear and compelling way.
- Ensure that our staff have the skills, knowledge and support to do their jobs.

The annual programme of inspections planned by HMICFRS is subject to approval by the Home Secretary, who may also request additional inspections if circumstances suggest this may be warranted: PCCs may also request specific inspections in their local areas. The Inspectorate also undertake thematic inspections and additional inspections where they consider that this is merited. The HMICFRS regularly carry out what are known as PEEL (Police effectiveness, efficiency and legitimacy) assessments as follows:

PEEL assessments

PEEL is an annual assessment of police forces in England and Wales. Forces are assessed on their effectiveness, efficiency and legitimacy. They are judged as outstanding, good, requires improvement or inadequate, on these categories (or pillars) based on inspection findings, analysis and Her Majesty's Inspectors' (HMIs) professional judgement across the year.

Each pillar has questions that focus on core areas of the work of the police. Judgements are applied to these questions.

Before 2018, every force received a separate report for each pillar. Reports were published by pillar, building up to an overall view of the force's performance at the end of the PEEL cycle.

From 2018/19 inspection year, the approach was changed to become more integrated. Each force now receives one report, providing a rounded assessment of its performance over the year. These reports are published in batches of 14 or 15 at a time. (HMICFRS 2018/19)

The standards of effectiveness, efficiency and legitimacy are classified as Outstanding, Good, Requires Improvement or Inadequate (categories that are shared with Ofsted). I found this system to be more transparent than in some of the other case studies: the justiceinspectorates.gov.uk website provides a clear chart of each police forces' performance on these three criteria – citizens can search using their own postcode, which leads to a link to their local force. Each specific report has an introduction providing a good summary in the form of the Chief Inspector's observations: here I provide one example from a positive report (West Yorkshire) and one from a more critical report (Greater Manchester) from the Justice Inspectorates website:

> I congratulate West Yorkshire Police on its excellent performance in keeping people safe and reducing crime.
>
> The force is good at preventing crime and anti-social behaviour. It works effectively with other agencies to identify and protect vulnerable people.
>
> The force is outstanding at planning for the future. I am impressed with its understanding of changing demand and how it links this to its financial planning and workforce development. Its leaders are ambitious and want to be at the forefront of innovative practice.
>
> It treats the public and its workforce fairly. And it continues to uphold an ethical culture and promote the standards of professional behaviour it expects.
>
> I am also particularly pleased with the force's performance in recording crime. It has substantially improved its crime recording accuracy since our last inspection.
>
> There remain some areas for improvement. It needs to improve the quality and supervision of criminal investigations, particularly those involving very vulnerable victims. The force also needs to increase its capability and capacity to effectively and proactively counter potential corruption within its workforce.

> Overall, I commend West Yorkshire Police for sustaining its positive performance over the past year. I am confident that it is well equipped for this to continue. (Phil Gormley, HM Inspector of Constabulary) (HMICFRS 2018/19)

The more critical commentary is as follows:

> I am satisfied with some of Greater Manchester Police's performance. But in some areas the force needs to make improvements.
>
> The force needs to improve how it prevents crime and anti-social behaviour. It needs to assure itself it has the capability and capacity to provide a consistent, effective neighbourhood policing service.
>
> The force is very good at dealing with serious and organised crime. But it needs to improve the quality and supervision of investigations into less serious crime. Following our last inspection, I was concerned that the force was inconsistent in how it responded to vulnerable people. I am disappointed that it hasn't fully addressed this. I remain concerned that the force may not be adequately protecting people at risk.
>
> The force needs to improve how it understands current and future demand. This should help it develop clear plans to make sure it uses its resources effectively.
>
> I am reassured that the force continues to uphold an ethical culture and promote standards of professional behaviour well.
>
> My overall assessment is that Greater Manchester Police's performance has declined since our last inspection. (Phil Gormley, HM Inspector of Constabulary) (HMICFRS 2018/19)

These summaries are succinct, clearly written and accessible – something that other organisations could learn from. They do provide the much sought after transparency – which I struggled to find in some of the other case studies. Of course, in the case of the police, there is no pretence of creating a market or an illusion of consumer choice.

We now explore the views and narratives of our police respondents: they have the perspective of senior officers who had experience of leading on inspections both internally and with partner organisations. Both the police respondents found the inspection demanding but also rewarding and providing an opportunity to demonstrate a high level of performance:

> In terms of the effort that was put into it, a significant amount. I had a number of staff working on one inspection for a number of weeks … we had to present a portfolio of evidence: the districts gathered the evidence and we put it all

together in a package. The inspectors come along for a week and triangulate the data. They undertake a series of interviews. It is resource intensive certainly in trying to provide the evidence that is required … it is very, very time consuming … unless you put in the effort it leads to a lower grading. Through the process it is possible to say, 'OK what is my action plan to achieve excellence?' There are things here we can do to improve. It is possible to achieve excellence and ask what my action plan is. You tend to maximise the available evidence and then to be creative in finding examples that are capable of showing evidence. The people doing this are middle grade and higher grade staff, as they are going to work hard and deliver. There is an incentive to be as creative as possible: if you cock it up not many other chances come along! (Respondent Nine)

Being inspected is a healthy thing to do and as a senior officer it didn't hold a lot of fear for me. It was a reflection of my performance and the performance of my team. (Respondent Ten)

As with the respondents in the other case studies, one respondent noted the variability of inspectors:

Some inspectors didn't have a good understanding … they sometimes don't understand the nuance as they were generalists and you would have to explain … that is just human nature. That was a challenge in terms of impact as you can't be an expert on everything. You can look at it like a royal burden upon us all and it was just extra work – or you can focus on where you need to get to if two is acceptable, then I looked at what you needed to do to get to one. (Respondent Nine)

There was some professional respect for the Lead Inspector, but again remarking variability within the team itself:

In general terms, yes, I would have professional respect certainly for the Lead Inspector: the Lead Inspector is a powerful figure and treated with a great degree of courtesy and respect. The team can be quite variable, so HMIC used to have permanent staff but now there is a varied associate model. Theoretically it is a better, a more bespoke team for a particular business area. (Respondent Nine)

The other respondent felt that the teams were more even and emphasised the sense of opportunity represented by an inspection:

Almost without exception [the inspectors] were respectful, courteous, reasonable: I had no issues with them at all. It is good experience as it is an opportunity to look at your organisation, it helps you identify issues in your organisation. (Respondent Ten)

Both respondents wanted to perform and to do well, but to do so was demanding of both time and effort:

> On what you need to do the grading criteria gave you a clue and helped to build an action plan and I did try to implement that. It is very challenging in terms of competing operational necessities. It is an ever moving feast – what was good last year is acceptable this year. It is a moving target – what is good and what is unacceptable. There are always things we can do to improve, so it is about attitude. (Respondent Nine)

> One of the really clever things for the inspectors to do is walk around and talk to the police constables and the sergeants. Of course I am going to pick the best staff for the focus groups. It was really powerful to walk around and check reality … the police are different from other organisations. If you are a PC or a sergeant you are not bothered about an inspection: you couldn't give a damn. This is not a criticism, I thought in the same way when I was in these ranks. I just wanted to get on with trying to give a good service without the unwelcome distraction of an inspection. (Respondent Ten)

There was also some frustration that inspections tend to underplay resource issues, citing an example where there was:

> reduced staffing from 1700 to 1200 – you reduce the resources, but hold it to the same or even higher standards. (Respondent Nine)

This respondent also placed a strong emphasis on resource issues and how this is underplayed during the inspection process:

> The truth is that there was just not enough available resources to effectively cover all the aspects of the service. The inspection teams in my view failed to take this into consideration. They didn't look holistically at the resources and as a result you could be constantly changing your service … you needed a more strategic view [from the Inspectorate]. (Respondent Ten)

> Compared to investigations from other agencies the level at which police are investigated is massively disproportionate and fundamentally wrong. For example, if a person dies in custody there would be many police officers suspended or placed on restricted duties. I have no real issue with this. However, compare this to a person who dies waiting in Accident and Emergency or in a mental health setting. It is highly likely that no one will be suspended or removed from duties. (Respondent Ten)

One respondent emphasised the opportunity for change provided by the inspection process:

In the police most inspections are thematic, looking at neighbourhood policing, safeguarding, CID, etc.: then you get a report and you make any changes that are needed. It helped me, for example, I wanted more staff working in vulnerability and child sexual exploitation but the Command Team didn't agree. They had understandable pressures from elected members and the public to maintain staffing levels in neighbourhood policing. The inspection identified that we needed more staff working in safeguarding so I took resources from neighbourhood policing. The inspection empowered me to do it even though the Assistant Chief Constable didn't really want it to happen. But then a different group of inspectors came back three months later and they said you are not doing enough on neighbourhood policing! (Respondent Ten)

I used the system to get things done before an inspection: when an inspection is due you get things done, in a supportive way so it is a win-win situation for the vulnerable. (Respondent Ten)

The respondents from the police were more positive about the inspection process than our other respondents: perhaps reflecting a more transparent system with no pretence of producing consumer choice or fake markets. They did, however, find the process demanding, frustrating, sometimes uneven and not always fit for purpose.

Joint inspections

Both police respondents had worked closely with partners on single agency or joint inspection processes and noted some important differences. One theme of this book is that inspection seemed to have a more visceral impact on social workers and teachers than on health staff, police officers or university staff, a proposal shared by our police respondents:

Teachers are really bruised by their system, I have seen people in schools not sleeping, at work 20 hours a day, it is all-consuming for them. (Respondent Nine)

In contrast, it is my view that a social worker or teacher views an inspection very differently. They do care about the findings and take the outcomes very personally. In the Police Service, PCs and sergeants didn't care too much about inspections, as it really made little difference to them. At this rank, most officers would not see a bad, or a good inspection, as a reflection on them. They would see it as a reflection on senior officers … Some of the social workers seemed scared in case one of their cases was chosen. (Respondent Ten)

This differential impact was organisational as well:

> There are examples of paranoia and paralysis around Ofsted inspections ... The effort and impact of inspections and the preparation in Children's Services is immense: my impression was that it brings almost the whole management to a grinding halt. It is difficult to understand from the outside but it is complete paralysis being created by the forthcoming Ofsted [inspection], a whole load of effort, posts being created. (Respondent Nine)

> The amount of time for preparation was immense compared to the police system. (Respondent Ten)

Both respondents were keen for partnership-based inspections to go well, as they respected the partner organisations, but also as it reflected on the respondents themselves professionally:

> I have a little bit of experience when partners are being inspected and some [experience of] interviews with Ofsted inspectors. It is a different experience as they are inspecting partners. There is pressure due to the perceived benefits of partnership. I put a lot of effort into the partnership, you wouldn't want to disrupt it. (Respondent Nine)

> For me as a Police Inspector in charge of partnerships I felt that the outcomes were partly a reflection on me: we are all in this together ... I believe I had a good working relationship with the partners. During one inspection an inspector asked me if I thought the working relationship with partners to safeguard children was good. I told an inspector that I had been talking to the Safeguarding Manager on the phone at 7 a.m. that very morning whilst still only in my underpants! We sorted out some urgent actions to safeguard a vulnerable missing child we were concerned about. We got outstanding! No one agency can do it on its own, it is all about partnership. (Respondent Ten)

The inspection process can be gamed, another theme of this book, to keep issues away from the inspectors or to expose issues if required:

> We disagree [with partners] behind closed doors: there is triangulation across partnerships. You can settle scores with a Director of Children's Services or [their assistant] if you have crossed swords. (Respondent Nine)

Partnership working was crucial to the respondents, but it had a value-based element beyond the reach of audit regimes, as in this example:

When I was a young cop there was [a run-down estate] where we faced violence and even got a TV thrown at us once! We got the council, the youth workers, and lots of other things in place. Five years later it was unrecognisable and a better place to live. It needed us to work together. (Respondent Ten)

The respondents were committed to the partnership inspections but noted the difference between Ofsted and the police inspection processes.

Policing and targets

As with many other of our case studies the police were subject to a target-led culture during the period of the British New Labour government (1997–2010). Both my police respondents, as we shall see, felt that targets had transformed policing, even beyond the actual existence of specific targets, thus agreeing with Muller's analysis in the USA:

the use of publicly released metrics to bolster the reputation of politicians and police chiefs has also created the incentives for gaming and fudging of numbers and for counter-productive diversion of effort. (2018: 126)

The New Labour approach was very explicit about the use of targets and the link with data:

The new performance management approach will also require: reliable statistical data to set targets otherwise they will lack credibility as a spur to improvement. (Home Office Strategic Plan 1999: 3.5.2)

Loveday outlines this development as follows:

To encourage this development, the strategic plan also requires the 'regular monitoring of performance against targets': 'information on comparative performance to help spread best practice': and the development of the capacity for audit and inspection to assess the performance of both agencies and the 'criminal justice system' as a whole (Strategic Plan, 3.5.2 and 3.5.3). The programme developed within the Strategic Plan is supported by objectives already identified by the 'Best Value' initiative. Within the efficiency plans required, the police will 'have to demonstrate they provide economic efficient effective and high quality services' (Strategic Plan, 4.7.5). Interestingly for the Government, the 'Best Value' approach, means that: 'The top priority is ensuring that police performance indicators are developed to capture whether police action is achieving objectives such as lower crime or increased confidence' (Strategic Plan, 4.7.5). (Loveday 2000: 218–19)

There are three specific factors worthy of discussion here: first, the use of discretion, second, the nature of crime prevention and third, the link between policing and level of criminality. Let us explore each in turn.

First, in the case of discretion – this refers to the ability of frontline staff to make decisions based on the specifics of each decision they deal with. For example, dropping litter is a crime, but the police do not charge most offenders: they tend to exercise their discretion. Crime and crime statistics are social constructions and do not simply exist out there waiting to be measured. The exercise of police discretion is the subject of much research and there is a whole language that developed around the use of discretion – 'crimeing' and 'culling' being amongst these. Crimeing is the process of deciding if something is a crime or not; culling is the process of hiding particular crimes by not identifying them as such. Thus, the link between actual recorded crime and real crime is constructed by a series of complex decision-making processes. Young produced a very complex and detailed study of police recording methods used to construct crime figures. He outlines his views on crime recording:

> Nearly every crime department I encountered at the time was engaged in the practice commonly known as 'culling'. This, in effect, means hiding or eliminating the incidence of reported crime from public scrutiny by tried and trusted means. At many police stations the crime book was locked away and only detectives were allowed to record crime. Detectable crimes were always welcome. However, many run of the mill minor crimes were often only collated on message pads or some other rough record and then only kept on the pad until it was suitable to ditch them. (Young 1991: 324)

Loveday followed up this study and concluded that:

> On the basis of limited yet still persuasive evidence, it would appear that any judgement of police efficiency made on the basis of crime clearance continues to be problematical. Nor, given what appear to be regular if not comprehensive police mis-classifications, are we able to conclude that crime rates in terms of particular types of offence are in fact falling. As interest within HMIC in integrity of recording offences has so clearly demonstrated, the police continue (as in the past) to use recording practices that enable them to give the appearance of achieving quite unrealistic levels of detection. (2000: 235)

Muller, again in the context of the USA, states that:

> massaging statistics had become 'ingrained in police culture': serious crimes such as robbery were downgraded to 'theft snatch', and rapes were often underreported so as to hit performance targets. (2018: 128)

These points are further illustrated by the difference between the British Crime Survey, which measures the public experience of crime and officially recorded crime. For example, the figures published in February 2021 illustrate that the public experienced more crime than that reported to the police:

> There have been fluctuations in the level of crime throughout 2020, particularly as the country went into lockdown and the later easing of restrictions; the [survey] estimated that there were approximately 11.7 million offences in the last 12 months ... Total police recorded crime decreased by 6% to approximately 5.7 million offences: this was driven by substantial falls during the April to June 2020 period, particularly in theft offences. (ONS 2021)

This specific situation is complicated by fluctuations during lockdowns caused by COVID-19 but the main point in the context of this study is that there is a difference between public experience (11.7 million crimes) and police recorded crime (5.7 million crimes). This difference illustrates the complexity of many of the metrics explored in this book: how do we construct the metrics that best reflect the actual incidence? Thus, the issue of discretion relates to the issue of targets. If targets are used (for example, a 20% decline in a particular crime) we have to take into account the use of discretion, the construction of the statistics and further the role of the police in crime prevention. Crime reduction is complex and multi-faceted and relates to factors such as the economic environment and situational crime prevention. For example, much has been written about the reduction of thefts of and from motor vehicles. Whilst research on this is complex there is no doubt that in England and Wales incidents peaked in 1992 and have declined steadily ever since: it is likely that this is linked to the introduction and development of electronic security devices, which is not actually connected to police activity. Causality is complex and multi-factoral, as suggested by the Home Office:

> Changes to policing, economic conditions, incarceration rates and long-term demographics may all have played some role, as may the timing of drug epidemics. (Home Office 2016: 10)

In an interview given on his retirement, Andy Cooke, former Chief Constable of Liverpool, perhaps surprisingly, analysed this issue as follows:

> The best crime prevention is increased opportunity and reduced poverty .... so there needs to be substantial funding into the infrastructure of our inner cities and our more deprived areas .... We need to reduce that deprivation and the scale of deprivation that we see in some of our communities, because if you give people a viable alternative, not all, but a lot will take it. (Dodd 2021)

Thus crime reduction is much more complex than setting a target for the police and this resulting in a reduction of crime:

> Public safety is only partially dependent on the effectiveness of the police. (Muller 2018: 125)

The respondents interviewed for this book appreciated that targets had a valuable, if limited role:

> You can look at that as a negative but it did drive improvement to a certain extent. (Respondent Nine)

> Some targets is really important: the 999 response time target for example is a really important target. If the response time is 20 minutes we need to know if we are meeting the target. If we are failing we need to understand why, so we can fix it. (Respondent Ten)

One of the respondents reflects as follows on the impact of the target culture:

> When I moved to [a different force] it was a target driven culture, the local government office were in touch with the targets .... You had to make the numbers look right like an accountancy model. There were a range of methods employed from the Blair/Blunkett regime, there was a lot of pressure on people. The Home Secretary wrote to the Chief Constable letters which were almost abusive, 'if you don't do this ...'. There was lots of short-termism driven by money, such as the street crime initiative. It changed with the Coalition government. They said no targets but actually by then the leadership were culturally wedded to targets. At the quarterly performance review with an Assistant Chief Constable they would dig into the depths of the district in terms of performance. It was fairly intrusive, assertive in terms of performance ... People were under a lot of pressure to make figures work – you can do it in a range of ethical or less ethical ways. (Respondent Nine)

This quote illustrates the impact of target culture – the existence of targets seeps deeply into the culture of organisations:

> Even then it became part of performance, they would send random surveys to an area and that would be translated into a performance score. If you were the inspector with the worse score then you were under pressure and probably wouldn't be inspector for very long. Then performance targets moved on: it did change the police culture. It had a personal impact, our Chief Constable was performance driven – but if it wasn't right you were in trouble. It really changed the culture: there was a lot of hokum around it. (Respondent Nine)

Respondents throughout this study refer to the divisive aspects of audit culture, a theme picked up as follows:

> For me with the targets I really objected to them when one team was played off against another. It was bean counting: how many arrests, stop and searches, traffic offences. As a middle manager I felt it was a wrong thing to do. I still feel strongly this way. (Respondent Ten)

Target culture was focused on things that could be measured to the detriment of more complex, less tangible areas, as this respondent argues:

> You couldn't measure vulnerability, you can't put it on a matrix, so it took away from vulnerability as we were focused on government targets on reducing burglaries, for example. If you were measuring arrests, stop and searches, traffic offences, then command may be inclined to cut resources on vulnerability: it was a very wrong thing to do. (Respondent Ten)

An important aspect of the audit culture in the police is the investigation of complaints: this is an important aspect of accountability for citizens. Prenzler and Porter (2016) argue that this issue is complex for three primary reasons, which include the wide range and diverse nature of claims made against the police, that the complaints may be vexatious and that the issues may have low visibility. Rowe (2020) notes that this issue of visibility has changed in recent years due to the use of body worn cameras by police officers. The system is overseen by the IOPC who outline their role as follows:

> The Independent Office for Police Conduct (IOPC) oversees the police complaints system in England and Wales. We investigate the most serious matters, including deaths following police contact, and set the standards by which the police should handle complaints. We use learning from our work to influence changes in policing.
>
> We are independent, and make our decisions entirely independently of the police and government. (policeconduct.gov.uk)

One of the respondents felt that this function fell out of the audit culture as such because:

> The Independent Office for Police Conduct is really separate to all this, they have twin roles, complaints and their own role as IOPC. (Respondent Nine)

The other respondent, perhaps unsurprising, expressed grave reservations about the IOPC:

> It is an absolute subject of frustration. In my opinion they are unprofessional and unconnected. Their investigations are too slow and they don't get the right messages out. (Respondent Ten)

This distrust meant that the work of the IOPC was not fully appreciated:

> They do publish thematic documents but, culturally, any good practice learning is not terribly well accepted. (Respondent Nine)

The high profile nature of these complaints adds a level to the complexity of police accountability.

Alternative scenarios

The police respondents were generally more positive about their direct experience of inspections than both our teaching and social work respondents. However, they had reflected on a more positive system aimed at organisational and professional development:

> Pre-supposing there is a need for an inspection system – we need to ask what we want it to achieve? It should be highlighting excellence and spreading good practice but it feels about being caught out – or on a technical point not reaching the appropriate grade. That is why it is attritional and creates paranoia. Grading systems like a star chart would be better rather the saying we are good, bad or inadequate. Can't we have something that measures improvement over time? There is politics at play, they need to hold public officials to account – and you can use the inadequate grading to do this. (Respondent Nine)

The other respondent wanted more realistic recommendations, a point made in Chapter 3 by our nurse respondents:

> The main issue about police inspections is that they are thematic but when they are making recommendations they need to look at the big picture, and be more realistic. (Respondent Ten)

This respondent felt that the inspection process had become detached from the crucial issue of resourcing, but fundamentally supported an inspection process:

All senior staff would like to do a good job in all areas, but we need more resources. Inspection should be a positive experience, some good comes out of inspections and I believe in it. (Respondent Ten)

CONCLUSION

Alternative forms of police accountability, and indeed the forms of service delivery, have been high profile since the emergence of the Black Lives Matters movement. We have seen that the police exist in a complex web of accountability, an accountability that is particularly important as the police exercise unique forms of power over citizens. The inspection system itself seemed to be more welcomed by our police respondents and more proportionate than in some of the other case studies, for example. Certainly the inspections were not greeted by the anxiety that is outlined by our social work and teacher respondents. The police respondents did have some reservations about the scale of inspection, the demands it makes and the disconnect from resource issues and challenges.

7

RETHINKING THE AUDIT CULTURE: TOWARDS AN ALTERNATIVE

The aim of this book has been to provide an extensive critique of audit, inspection and measurement in the public sector, what we have referred to as the audit culture. Muller summarises the audit culture succinctly as follows:

> The belief that it is possible and desirable to replace judgment, acquired by personal experience and talent, with numerical indicators of comparative performance based upon standardized data (metrics)
>
> The belief that making such metrics public (transparent) assures that institutions are actually carrying out their purposes (accountability)
>
> The belief that the best way to motivate people within these organisations is by attaching rewards and penalties to their measured performance, rewards that are either monetary (pay-for-performance) or reputational (rankings). (2018: 6)

We have drawn on the work of Jerry Muller, Mike Power and Onora O'Neill amongst others, who encourage us to see audit measures as narratives and as constructions based in a lack of trust, rather than as straightforward statements of fact. Redden argues that audit measurements are indeed a:

> social fabrication at every step – conducted by tendentious agents with unstable consequences in institutional environments shaped by multiple forces, power relations and knowledge. (2019: 113)

We have seen the meaning of this quote from Redden unfold throughout our five case studies in this book: we have witnessed that the audit culture sometimes has negative intended and unintended consequences. We have addressed and hopefully provided evidence around three key issues throughout the text:

1. Audit culture is based in a lack of trust in public service professionalism and has undermined what used to be seen as the public service ethos.

2. Audit culture produces proxy measures which become fetishised and can have a negative impact on service delivery.

3. The attempt to 'quantify' the 'quality' of public service organisations is expensive, diversionary, leads to 'gaming' and can cause distress to many well-motivated professionals.

Evidence to address these issues has been drawn from the academic and the grey literature, from the author's study of official sources and from the respondents interviewed for this book. In this final chapter we move on to explore the alternative narratives around this dominant set of believes. As Downe argued in 2008, and which remains largely the case in the contemporary environment:

> There has been almost no public debate about alternatives to the inspection pro-
> cess, but there are other approaches. A range of peer review initiatives, 'learning
> networks' and benchmarking clubs have been in place for some time. (2008: 32)

The case for an alternative will be summarised here and will provide a moral, value-based case for reform and also a practical case for reform: we then move on to suggest some alternative directions for the future. The social commentator George Monbiot argues that change and reform are driven by narratives:

> Stories are the means by which we navigate the world. They allow us to inter-
> pret its complex and contradictory signals. We all possess a narrative instinct: an
> innate disposition to listen for an account of who we are and where we stand.
> (Monbiot 2017b)

and further that alternative scenarios require new narratives to emerge such as:

> Through restoring community, renewing civic life and claiming our place in the
> world, we build a society in which our extraordinary nature – our altruism, empa-
> thy and deep connection – is released. A kinder world stimulates and normal-
> ises our kinder values. I propose a name for this story: the Politics of Belonging.
> (Monbiot 2017b)

We agree with this argument and attempt to think through how this approach can apply to challenging the audit culture. Here, we make the case for alterna-tive approaches to challenge the power of dominant narrative: thus contributing to building a kinder organisational network as suggested by Monbiot. The case will be made for trust to replace the narrative of risk, blame and failure with a positive public service ethos: there are two aspects we go on to explore here: a moral case and practical case.

THE MORAL CASE

Throughout this book we have seen the impact of the audit culture: we have heard from professionals who felt undermined, depressed and damaged by the process. The case is made here for a public service ethos – that is that a commitment to public service should be emphasised in training, by professional associations and by government. The emphasis on targets and outcomes has arguably undermined this value base – the jobs of public sector professionals have become more about meeting a technical, measurable outcome rather than the ethos of service based in collective values. Words such as kindness, responsiveness, flexibility and caring could and should replace the dominance of targets, outcomes and gradings. In summary, we can say that trust can replace audit as a dominant approach to, and within, the public sector. One objection to this may be that we cannot always trust public servants – we can think of medical staff who have failed patients, how police officers have failed minority groups, teachers who have abused their position of power and so on. How can we trust people like this? But, of course, all this poor, and sometimes dangerous practice has taken place *within a dominant audit culture*, often in organisations that had recently achieved successful inspections. We can conclude that audit culture is not the answer to poor practice. Mike Power quotes Brathwaite as arguing that government inspectors, 'ensure the quality of your records, not the quality of your deeds' (1997: 131). In any case, monitoring and disciplinary procedures are already in place to tackle poor practice in all the organisations we have explored here. A shift towards trust-based approaches could revitalise the public sector towards a set of practices based in morality, in values and in commitment, thus displacing paranoia and anxiety about inspection and audit outcomes. As Marquand argued:

> In a sense true of no previous society, each of us depends, every day of every week, on the dedication and sense of responsibility of professionally skilled people. (1990: 18)

THE PRACTICAL CASE

Throughout this book we have also made a practical case for a change to the dominant audit culture. We have outlined examples of high costs, of unintended consequences, of gaming and of distortions of practice, in summary:

The overload of accountability demands undermines productivity, responsiveness, and service quality. (Halachmi 2014: 560)

Audit culture changes behaviour, we would argue often in a detrimental manner:

The behaviour of workers comes to reflect the incentives and sanctions implicit in those measurements. (Lipsky 1980: 51)

By changing the audit culture there would be clear benefits: organisations could focus more on the task in hand, rather than on data gathering and preparation for inspection. A change of culture would free financial resources for public service and encourage inspectors to have a more direct, supportive, developmental link to practice. The potential benefits are significant and could make a considerable difference to the public sector: in addition we could free up the human and financial resources to develop public services. The considerable expertise of the inspectors could themselves be utilised in direct practice and in working as mentors and advisors for frontline professionals. The suggestions in this chapter are in the spirit of the approach suggested in O'Neill in her 2002 BBC Reith lecture:

Let me share my sense of some of the possibilities. Intelligent accountability, I suspect, requires more attention to good governance and fewer fantasies about total control. Good governance is possible only if institutions are allowed some margin for self-governance of a form appropriate to their particular tasks, within a framework of financial and other reporting. (2002: 58)

DEVELOPING AN ALTERNATIVE

It is suggested here that the inspection process could be rethought around the following themes:

- inspection through partnership
- building on trust in professionals
- re-establishing a public sector ethos
- enhanced democratic involvement
- developing peer review.

Inspection through partnership

The least radical alternative would be to keep much of the current system but to make it a kinder, more empathetic, more partnership-based service. I have personal experience of this through a predecessor of Ofsted and the Care Quality Commission – the Social Service Inspectorate. The inspectors explored the child protection system in the area I was responsible for and found some strengths but also some weaknesses, namely not fully involving parents and carers in the process. They shared models for enhancing parental involvement in child protection case conferences and worked with us on this. I found the process helpful, motivating and positive – the opposite of the narrative explained by some of the respondents in this book. At the time of writing this book there is some evidence that Ofsted, under the leadership of Amanda Spielman, is moving towards this more developmental model.

Building trust on professionals

Public trust in most professionals is relatively high: 81% in the case of judges, for example. Amongst the lowest rates of trust are in government ministers (17%), advertising executives (17%) and lowest of all politicians (14%) (Ipsos MORI: 2019). For the professions relevant to this study levels of trust are high: over 90% for doctors and nurses, 89% for teachers, 84% for professors and 76% for the police. The nature of this trust has changed over the decades. In the nineteenth century trust in vicars, doctors and teachers arose from the fact that they held simply these posts: such people were de facto to be trusted and were mainly known through personal contact. There were perhaps two challenges to this trust during the twentieth century. The first came from intellectuals and from the left. In the 1960s writers such as Fanon, Illich, Foucault and Goffman challenged institutions such as mental asylums and schools. The so-called common sense position that schools exist simply to educate people, or that asylums to cure people, was challenged helping to raise questions about the role of professionals. A second and perhaps more profound challenge came from a range of scandals and public inquiries that examined the role of a wide-range of professionals – such as police officers, social workers, doctors and nurses. Some significant inquiries, including the date of publication, are listed below:

- the inquiry into Beverley Allitt, a nurse (1994)
- the inquiry into the death of Stephen Lawrence (1999)
- the inquiry into Dr Harold Shipman, a GP (2002)
- the inquiry into the death of 'Baby Peter' (2010)
- the inquiry into Dr Ian Paterson, a doctor (2020).

It is beyond the scope of this book to examine these in detail (see Butler and Drakeford 2005; Jones 2014) but no doubt they, collectively, undermined elements of trust in professionals. Some may use these examples to argue for a stronger audit culture, but of course they all took place within the types of powerful audit regimes explored in this book. We can argue for a system based in trust where we start from trust and build audits regimes that assume the best rather than the worst.

Re-establishing a public sector ethos

Rebuilding a public sector ethos should be fundamental to any rethinking: building services not on measurement or targets but on a public sector driven by service and values. In the United Kingdom there are established ways of working towards this through what are known as the Nolan Principles: selflessness, integrity, objectivity, accountability, openness, honesty and leadership. The latter is perhaps on a different level, the first six provide a sound basis for working in the type of institutions explored in the book. It has become unfashionable to use phrases such as I want to help people or I want to make a difference: these types of motivation should and could become central to public service and displace competition, league tables, outcomes and targets. Peters (2014), drawing on the work of Friedrich, argues that:

> no amount of control could protect against individuals or organisation that did not have the appropriate values ... the only real protection against malfeasance was the training of public servants and the inculcation of values into the public service. (2014: 216)

Democratic involvement

In many ways inspection norms and national standards work against local democracy. If every Director of Children's Services wants to achieve the best report against current Ofsted standards then what is the role of local democracy? As Davis and Martin argue:

> The place shaping agenda advocated by the Lyons Inquiry ... throws the potential conflict between national priorities and what matters locally and politically into sharper relief. It is difficult to see how a standard set of performance criteria, of the kind which have been used in inspection frameworks over the last decade, will survive as localities are increasingly encouraged to shape their own priorities and one size cannot therefore any longer fit them all. (2008: 146)

More theoretically Mike Power sees audit as a mask and as an accountable technique and therefore:

> Audit is in this respect a substitute for democracy rather than its aid. (1997: 127)

The term postcode lottery has become a negative but actually a sense of place, diversity and difference suggests that variation according to local needs and related decision-making can be seen as a democratic plus. As in the Finnish policy, explored in Chapter 4, which involved the abolition of their national inspection body, such a move can encourage local place-based, democratic decision-making.

There are various levels of citizen involvement which could be drawn on. Damgaard and Lewis (2014) draw on Arnstein's model of participation: five levels of accountability moving from education, to involvement, advice, collaboration and, at the highest level of participation, to joint ownership. Angela Rayner, in the context of the Labour Party, put the following case for a more democratic approach to regulation in higher and further education:

> Labour must abolish all market-based systems of accountability such as Ofsted in FE and the Teaching and Research Excellence Frameworks in HE. In their place, Labour should create a national regulatory body for tertiary education – intrinsically linked and co-operating with a similar body in compulsory education – that can allocate funding according to a national education strategy informed by robust and democratic feedback mechanisms. This body should have an elected board, with representation reflecting fairly the mutual interests in tertiary education: academics, teachers, administrators, parents and communities, students, trade unions, civil servants, and Members of Parliament from all political parties. (Marketisation of Higher Education 2019)

There are further, even more radical models for this, which could build on a Brazilian model championed by George Monbiot:

> In the Brazilian city of Porto Alegre … about 20 per cent of the municipal budget ….. is allocated by the people. The process begins with public meetings that are used to review the previous year's budget and elect local representatives to the new budget council. Working with the people of their districts, these representatives agree local priorities, which are then submitted to the budget council. The council weights the distribution of money according to local levels of poverty and lack of infrastructure. In Porto Alegre, around 50,000 people are typically involved in the development of a budget. (Monbiot 2017a)

Whilst Monbiot is addressing a wider canvas than the one explored in this book it can be argued that the principles can be applied to the democratisation of organisational accountability.

Peer review

One substitute for the dominance of the current audit culture is an enhanced form of peer review – these systems already exist in some of the organisations explored. The system can run as follows:

- Each relevant organisation forms a panel of peer reviewers, representing different layers and forms of expertise within the organisation, forming a peer review panel. These panels could include citizens, who are users of the service, sometimes referred to as experts by experience.
- Peer review panels are allocated to review another organisation. No fee would be payable as each organisation would provide and receive the service in turn.
- The receiving organisation presents any background documentation required by the process.
- The panel is then hosted for, say, a week and undertakes meetings with professionals and service users.
- The peer review panel then produces a report emphasising any strengths and weaknesses found during the process.
- The receiving organisation then produces an action plan based on the report: a follow-up review can take place as required.

The advantages of such a system are that it would be less demanding of resources, led by people with current day-to-day experience, combined with more democratic representation and therefore it would lead to a more empathetic, kinder and more developmental approach.

CONCLUSION

It is hoped that this book has critically explored the dominance of the audit culture in the United Kingdom in the twenty-first century. We have heard authentic voices from those immersed in this dominant culture and critically explored many official sources. Theoretical guidance has been provided by Mike Power, Onora O'Neill and Jerry Muller, amongst others. These theoretical frameworks have been supplemented by anecdotes and experiences, which hopefully contribute towards a counter-narrative to the dominant audit culture. We have tentatively suggested some alternative ways forward – moving towards a more empathetic culture that can support, develop, and contribute to learning and hold to account to the public where necessary.

REFERENCES

Adab, P., Rouse, A.M., Mohammed, M.A. and Marshall, T. (2002) Performance league tables: the NHS deserves better. *British Medical Journal,* 324 (7329): 95–98.

Barnett, A.G. and Moher, D. (2019) Turning the tables: A university league-table based on quality not quantity. *F1000Research,* 8: 583.

Bassey, M. (2020) *Letter to the Guardian,* 7.2.2020.

Bennett, R.J. and Robinson, S.L. (2000) Development of a measure of workplace deviance. *Journal of Applied Psychology,* 85(3): 349.

Britton, P. (2020) Greater Manchester Police chief constable Ian Hopkins resigns. *Manchester Evening News,* 18 December. Available at: www.manchester-eveningnews.co.uk/news/greater-manchester-news/ian-hopkins-quits-gmp-police-19485781 (accessed 27 May 2021).

Burgess, N. (2019) Ban school league tables. *The Guardian,* 26.01.2019.

Butler, I. and Drakeford, M. (2005) *Scandal, Social Policy and Social Welfare.* Bristol: Policy Press.

Cheng, J.H. and Marsh, H.W. (2010) National Student Survey: Are differences between universities and courses reliable and meaningful? *Oxford Review of Education,* 36(6): 693–712.

Collini, S. (2012) *What Are Universities For?* London: Penguin.

Coughlan, S. (2020) Schools warned against 'gaming' exam league tables. BBC News, 21 January. Available at: www.bbc.co.uk/news/education-51194249 (accessed 27 May 2021).

Cowburn, A. (2020) A level results: Gavin Williamson facing backlash. *The Independent,* 13.8.2020.

Cui, V., French, A. and O'Leary, M. (2019) A missed opportunity? How the UK's teaching excellence framework fails to capture the voice of university staff. *Studies in Higher Education,* DOI: 10.1080/03075079.2019.1704721.

Damgaard, B. and Lewis, J. (2014) Citizen participation in public accountability. In Bovens, M., Goodin, R.E. and Schillemans, T. (eds), *The Oxford Handbook of Public Accountability.* Oxford: Oxford University Press, pp. 258–272.

Davis, H. and Martin, S. (2008) The future of public services inspection. In Davis, H. and Martin, S. (eds), *Public Services Inspection in the UK.* London: Jessica Kingsley Publishers, pp. 135–151.

Dennis, M. and Laporte, N. (2014) *The Stasi: Myth and Reality.* London: Routledge.

Dodd, V. (2021) Tackle poverty and inequality to reduce crime. *The Guardian,* 18.4.2021.

Downe, J. (2008) Inspection of local government services. In Davis, H. and Martin, S. (eds), *Public Services Inspection in the UK*. London: Jessica Kingsley Publishers, pp. 19–36.

Dubnick, M. (2014) Accountability as a cultural keyword. In Bovens, M., Goodin, R.E. and Schillemans, T. (eds), *The Oxford Handbook of Public Accountability*. Oxford: Oxford University Press, pp. 23–38.

EDSK (2019) *Requires Improvement: The Future of Ofsted and School Inspection*. London: EDSK.

Ferguson, D. (2019) 'If you get a good inspector, it can be magic': Is Labour right to want Ofsted gone? *The Guardian*, 1.10.2019.

Ferguson, H., Gibson, M. and Plumbridge, G. (2019) Independent Evaluation of the Implementation of Ofsted's Framework for Inspection of Local Authority Children's Services (ILACS). Department of Social Work and Social Care, University of Birmingham.

Foucault, M. (1997) Ethics: Subjectivity and truth. *Essential Works of Michel Foucault, 1954–1984. Vol. 1*. New York: New Press.

Frankham, J. (2017) Employability and higher education: The follies of the 'Productivity Challenge' in the Teaching Excellence Framework. *Journal of Education Policy*, 32(5): 628–641.

Frost, N. (2021) *Safeguarding Children and Young People*. London: Sage.

Gibbons, A. and Roberts, J. (2020) Inspections can add to teacher stress, says Ofsted. *TES*, 21 January. Available at: www.tes.com/news/inspections-can-add-teacher-stress-says-ofsted (accessed 27 May 2021).

Goffman, F. (1978) *The Presentation of Self in Everyday Life*. London: Penguin.

Gogol, N. (2014) *The Government Inspector and Other Works*. Hertfordshire: Wordsworth.

The Guardian (2014) Secret Teacher: Why are we really put through the pain of Ofsted inspections? 24 May. Available at: www.theguardian.com/teacher-network/teacher-blog/2014/may/24/secret-teacher-ofsted-inspections-education (accessed 27 May 2021).

Halachmi, A. (2014) Accountability overload. In Bovens, M., Goodin, R.E. and Schillemans, T. (eds), *The Oxford Handbook of Public Accountability*. Oxford: Oxford University Press, pp. 258–272.

Hamel, M.B., Roland, M. and Campbell, S. (2014) Successes and failures of pay for performance in the United Kingdom. *The New England Journal of Medicine*, 370(20): 1944–1950.

HMICFRS (2018) Our purpose, values and objectives. Available at: www.justiceinspectorates.gov.uk/hmicfrs/about-us/purpose-values-objectives/ (accessed 27 May 2021).

HMICFRS (2018/19) PEEL assessments. Available at: www.justiceinspectorates.gov.uk/hmicfrs/peel-assessments/peel-2018/ (accessed 27 May 2021).

HM Treasury (2020) *Public Expenditure*. London: HMG.

Home Office (1999) *Home Office Strategic Plan*. London: HMG.

Home Office (2016) *Reducing Criminal Opportunity*. London: Home Office.

Hood, R., Grant, R., Jones, R. and Goldacre, A. (2016) A study of performance indicators and Ofsted ratings in English child protection services. *Children and Youth Services Review*, 67: 50–56.

Hood, R., Nilsson, D. and Habibi, R. (2019) An analysis of Ofsted inspection reports for children's social care services in England. *Child & Family Social Work*, 24(2): 227–237.

House, R. (2020) *Pushing Back to Ofsted: Safeguarding and the Legitimacy of Ofsted's Inspection Judgements – A Critical Case Study*. Stroud: InterActions.

Ingram, J., Elliott, V., Morin, C., Randhawa, A. and Brown, C. (2018) Playing the system: Incentives to 'game' and educational ethics in school examination entry policies in England. *Oxford Review of Education*, 44(5): 545–562.

Ipsos Mori. (2019) *Veracity Index*. London: Ipsos Mori.

Ipsos Mori. (2020) *Veracity Index*. London: Ipsos Mori.

Jones, R. (2014) *The Story of Baby P*. Bristol: Policy.

King's Fund (2005) *An Independent Audit of the NHS Under Labour (1997–2005)*. London: King's Fund.

Labour Party (2019) *Labour Party Manifesto*. London: Labour Party.

Leckie, G. and Goldstein, H. (2010) The limitations of using school league tables to inform school choice. Unpublished.

Leckie, G. and Goldstein, H. (2019) The importance of adjusting for pupil background in school value-added models: A study of Progress 8 and school accountability in England. *BERA – British Educational Research Journal*, 45: 518–537.

Lightfoot, L. (2020) Outstanding primary schools fail Ofsted inspections under sudden rule switch. *The Guardian*, 4.2.2020.

Lipsky, M. (1980) *Street-Level Bureaucracy*. New York: Russell Sage Foundation.

Loveday, B. (2000) Managing crime: Police use of crime data as an indicator of effectiveness. *International Journal of the Sociology of Law*, 28(3): 215–237.

Macfarlane, B. and Tomlinson, M. (2017) Critiques of student engagement. *Higher Education Policy*, 30(1): 5–21.

Machin, S. (2011) Houses and schools: Valuation of school quality through the housing market. *Labour Economics*, 18(6) 723–729.

Magee, H., Davis, L.J. and Coulter, A. (2003) Public views on healthcare performance indicators and patient choice. *Journal of the Royal Society of Medicine*, 96(7): 338–342.

Marketisation of Higher Education (2019) Self-regulation and public ownership in tertiary education. Available at: https://hemarketisation.wordpress.com/2019/07/01/self-regulation-and-public-ownership-in-tertiary-education/ (accessed 267 May 2021).

Marmot, M., Allen, J., Boyce, T., Goldblatt, P. and Morrison, J. (2020) *Health Equity in England: The Marmot Review Ten Years On*. London: Institute of Health Equity.

Marquand, D. (1990) Smashing times. *New Statesman and Society*. 27.7.1990.

Miller, P. and Rose, N. (1992) Political power beyond the state: Problematics of government. *British Journal of Sociology*, 42(2): 173–205.

Monbiot, G. (2017a) Becoming unstoppable. Available at: www.monbiot.com/2017/11/02/becoming-unstoppable/ (accessed 27 May 2021).

Monbiot, G. (2017b) How do we get out of this mess? *The Guardian*, 9.9.2017.

Monbiot, G. (2019) *Out of the Wreckage*. Harmondsworth: Penguin.

Moore, R. (2021) The free-market gamble: Has Covid broken UK universities? *The Observer*, 17.1.2021.

Morris, S., Sutton, M. and Gravelle, H. (2005) Inequity and inequality in the use of health care in England: An empirical investigation. *Social Science and Medicine*, 60(6): 1251–1266.

Muller, J. (2018) *The Tyranny of Metrics*. Princeton: Princeton University Press.

National Health Service (2021) *NHS Constitution for England*. London: DH&SC.

Neary, M. (2016) Teaching Excellence Framework: A critical response and an alternative future. *Journal of Contemporary European Research*, 12(3): 690–695.

NEU (2019) Ofsted inspection – advice for members on the main or upper pay range. Available at: https://neu.org.uk/advice/ofsted-inspection-advice-members-main-or-upper-pay-range (accessed 27 May 2021).

Nursing Times (2014) New data reveals patient mortality rates for individual surgeons. Available at: www.nursingtimes.net/clinical-archive/perioperative-nursing/new-data-reveals-patient-mortality-rates-for-individual-surgeons-19-11-2014/ (accessed 27 May 2021).

Office for Students (2016) *London School of Economics TEF submission*. London: OfS.

Office for Students (2019) *TRAC Guidance: The Transparent Approach to Costing for UK Higher Education Institutions*. Office for Students. Available at: www.trac.ac.uk/wp-content/uploads/2019/07/TRAC-Guidance-v2.4.pdf (accessed 27 May 2021).

Ofsted (2006) *Joint Area Review of London Borough of Haringey Children's Services*. London: Ofsted.

Ofsted (2008) *Joint Area Review of Haringey Children's Services Authority Area*. London: Ofsted.

Ofsted (2017) *Annual Teachers Survey*. London: Ofsted.

Ofsted (2019) *Inspection of Local Authority Children's Services Framework Implementation Review*. London: Ofsted.

O'Neill, O. (2002) *A Question of Trust?* Cambridge: Cambridge University Press.

ONS (2021) Crime in England and Wales: Year ending September 2020. Statistical Bulletin. Available at: www.ons.gov.uk/peoplepopulationandcommunity/crimeandjustice/bulletins/crimeinenglandandwales/yearendingseptember2020 (accessed 27 May 2021).

Patterson, J. (2015) Five reasons the Teaching Excellence Framework is bad news for higher education. Available at: https://blogs.lse.ac.uk/impactofsocialsciences/2015/09/10/five-reasons-the-teaching-excellence-framework-is-bad-news-for-higher-education/ (accessed 27 May 2021).

Peters, B. (2014) Accountability in public administration. In Bovens, M., Goodin, R.E. and Schillemans, T. (eds), *The Oxford Handbook of Public Accountability*. Oxford: Oxford University Press, pp. 211–225.

Power, M. (1997) *The Audit Society: Rituals of Verification*. Oxford: Clarendon.

Prenzler, T. and Porter, L. (2016) Improving police behaviour and police-community relations through innovative responses to complaints. In Lister, S. and Rowe, M. (eds), *Accountability of Policing*. London: Routledge, pp. 49–68.

Redden, G. (2019) *Questioning Performance Measurement*. London: Sage.

REF2021 (2020) Index of Revisions to the 'Guidance on Submissions' (2019/01). Available at: www.ref.ac.uk/media/1447/ref-2019_01-guidance-on-submissions. pdf (accessed 27 May 2021).

Rosling, H. (2018) *Factfulness.* London: Hodder and Stoughton.

Rowe, M. (2020) *Policing the Police: Challenges of Democracy and Accountability.* Bristol: Policy Press.

Sandel, M. (2020) *The Tyranny of Merit: What's Become of the Common Good?* London: Allen Lane.

Sayer, D. (16th Dec, 2015a) The research excellence framework. *The Guardian.*

Sayer, D. (2015b) *Rank Hypocrisies.* London: Sage.

Schools Week (2020) Reform league tables to include pupil wellbeing, says ASCL. Available at: https://schoolsweek.co.uk/reform-league-tables-to-include-pupil-wellbeing-says-ascl/ (accessed 27 May 2021).

Taylor-Gooby, P. (2009) *Reframing Social Citizenship.* Oxford: Oxford University Press.

Thompson, E.P. (1970) *Warwick University Limited.* Harmondsworth: Penguin.

The Times (2013) Gove to overhaul GCSE league tables to stop schools 'gaming' the system. Available at: https://www.thetimes.co.uk/article/gove-to-overhaul-gcse-league-tables-to-stop-schools-gaming-the-system-wwlxv2b6sn9 (accessed 27 May 2021).

Turner, A. (2019) Academics voice concerns over What Works Centre's family group conferences study. *Community Care* 3 June.

UCU (n.d.) *Discoveries that Would Not Survive the REF.* Available at: www.ucu.org. uk/media/3591/Discoveries-that-would-not-survive-the-REF/pdf/ucu_notsurviv-ingtheREF_r1.pdf (accessed 27 May 2021).

Vainikainen, M.P., Thuneberg, H., Marjanen, J., Hautamäki, J., Kupiainen, S. and Hotulainen, R. (2017) How do Finns know? Educational monitoring without inspection and standard setting. In Blömeke, S. and Gustafsson, J.E. (eds), *Standard Setting in Education: The Nordic Countries in an International Perspective.* Cham: Springer, pp. 243–259.

Warren, M. (2014) Accountability and democracy. In Bovens, M., Goodin, R.E. and Schillemans, T. (eds), *The Oxford Handbook of Public Accountability.* Oxford: Oxford University Press, pp. 39–54.

Wheale, S. (2019) Top of the class: Labour seeks to emulate Finland's school system. *The Guardian.* 27.9.2019.

Wilby, P. (2018) The profile: Amanda Speilman. *The Guardian,* 6.2.2018.

YouGov (2019) *Teachers' Awareness and Perceptions of Ofsted.* Teacher Attitude Survey.

Young, M. (1991) *An Inside Job: Policing and Police Culture.* Clarendon Press, Oxford.

INDEX